NORM! CLARKE♠!

Sin City's Ace Insider

1,000 Naked Truths

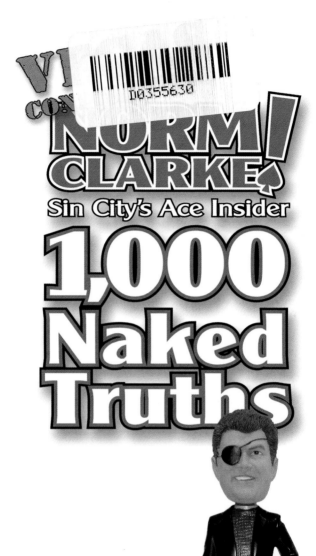

NORM!

Cataloguing-in-Publication Data Available

ISBN #1-932173-26-9

Stephens
Press LLC

A Stephens Media Group Company
PO Box 1600
Las Vegas, Nevada 89125-1600
702-387-5260 / 702-387-2997 FAX

www.stephenspress.com

Dedication

For Frank Wright

Without Frank, our community has a gaping void. Frank, curator of the Nevada State Museum & Historical Society, was one of the first people I contacted when I started this book. You'll find his contribution of key dates in Las Vegas history in the history chapter, but he helped in so many other ways.

Acknowledgments

Everyone has a book in them, the saying goes. This one has been spinning around in *Las Vegas Review-Journal* publisher Sherm Frederick's mind for some time. I just happened to walk in his door at the right time.

It was August 1999 and I was in the *Review-Journal* publisher's office to sell him on the idea of hiring me as the paper's first gossip columnist in several decades. But at some point during our conversation, Sherm started selling me, and the book idea became one of his pitching points: "There's a great opportunity for a top 10 tourist guidebook here and I think it would fit perfectly with the column."

I am not the first journalist to give in to this city's gravitational pull. I was in Frederick's office that Monday morning because I was convinced that Las Vegas was the ultimate buffet for a "three-dot" columnist. Twenty years earlier, I had worked in the *R-J* newsroom as a roving reporter for The Associated Press out of San Diego and Los Angeles. The Las Vegas AP office was surely one of its smallest anywhere in the world. Not much larger than a walk-in closet, it was glass-enclosed with a view of the newsroom. On many an assignment to Las Vegas, I observed Forrest Duke, never without his Los Angeles Dodgers cap, entering the newsroom to drop off his entertainment column. A thunderbolt hit me. "Now that," I vividly recall thinking, "would be a great job."

Two decades later, I got my chance.

Sherm's book idea was the clincher. Barely a month later I traded my 27th-floor downtown Denver condo with its blood-red Rocky Mountain sunsets for a view of The Strip and its blazing neon. After 15 years as a sports reporter, sports columnist and the man-about-town columnist, all at the *Rocky Mountain News*, I was leaving for the perfect job for those of us who love history and storytelling.

The first lists were created 18 months later, on Valentine's Day 2001 (some of us have no life) and by September, some 85 lists were completed. Then 9-11 changed the world. The book project was put on hold.

A few months later, a kidney stone attack led to the discovery of prostate cancer and, with it, more changed priorities.

I am humbly appreciative of this city's many dedicated medical professionals. Heartfelt thanks to Dr. Alan Demby, for urging a PSA test and his care when complications continued; to Dr. Steven Miller for taking charge when my legs inexplicably stopped working for three months; to Cathy Champlin and her dedicated crew at Heathsouth, for teaching me how to walk again, and to the skillful Dr. Sina Nasri for taking care of a thyroid condition that caused the mass production of kidney stones at a time when I was trying to recover from all the other surgeries.

I am deeply grateful to Sherm for the opportunity to be part of this Golden Era of Las Vegas. I wouldn't have made the move without the encouragement and blessing of my brother Jeff Scheid, now director of photography at the *R-J*, and his wife Jenny. Their continuous support and friendship means the world to me.

I am indebted to *R-J* editor Tom Mitchell and staff

for their professionalism, especially the night shift for shoe-horning all those late-night sightings into an already over-length column. I'm sure they would all agree my epitaph should read, "I love deadlines. I like the whooshing sound they make as they fly by" (Thank you, Douglas Adams).

My thanks to Carolyn Uber, a true professional who oversaw this project for Stephens Press with verve and vision, and to gifted colleague Mike Weatherford and his wife Joan for their superb editing and painstaking research. If you love Las Vegas, Mike's *Cult Vegas* is must reading.

Many friends, upon hearing about the book, contributed numerous ideas. Felix Rappaport, president and chief operating officer of New York-New York, offered so many over lunch one day that I got writer's cramp. Ditto for Mike Fleeman of *People* magazine.

During my recovery and throughout this project, I thanked my lucky stars that I had friends like Robin Leach, Denny Rue, Denny and Melanie Dressman, Rhonda Michotte, Ned Fairchild and Marilyn Michotte, Andy Lippman, Byron Yake, Randy Rutherford, Andrew and Denise Hudson, Drew and Debbie Litton, Deb Goeken, Mark Wolf, Doug Elfman, Barry Forbis, Mark and Tammy Dyer, the late Joe Stein, and Halina Akonom. Without AP pals Paul Freeman and the late Wick Temple, my old coach Ray Frank and surrogate dad Gordie and Alice Spear of the *Miles City Star* (Montana), I'd still be delivering groceries somewhere in Montana. I am hugely grateful to Joanne Downey, *Review-Journal* promotions and events manager, Deke Castleman and Anthony Curtis at Huntington Press for their significant input and contributions.

Much appreciation goes to Sue Campbell, the book designer who read my last minute illegible notes; to Chris Wheeler, cover designer; and to the Stephens Press team — Yvonne Simmons, Thom

Pruitt, Zabrina Rapozo, and Krista Morgan.

And would I ever be remiss in not thanking the many nameless "spies" — publicists, valets, cocktail servers, bartenders, and service industry types — whose contributions to my column, and this book, are immense.

Special thanks, too, to my pals who chipped in with lists: Don Usherson, Ira David Sternberg, former *R-J.* gaming writer Jeff Simpson, Tim Dahlberg, Al Bernstein, George Knapp, Robin Leach, Ernie Cheong, Bobby Barrett, and Rob Johnson. And to Cara Roberts, aka the Leggy Blonde, who bailed me out in more ways than one with her wit and wisdom.

Norm Clarke
Las Vegas, Summer 2004

Author's Note

This book was compiled and written without the solicitation of any advertisements or considerations. No payments of any kind were received from any entity or person mentioned in the book.

The selections, for the most part, were based on my own research along with input from colleagues and respected food and entertainment devotees. When applicable, most lists are in alphabetical order and should not be construed as a 1-through-10 ranking or an endorsement of the service or goods offered. The opinions expressed are strictly my own.

Contents

Chapter 2
Celebrity City

Chapter 3
Sin City

Chapter 4
Where To Eat

Chapter 5
Entertainment Today

Chapter 6
Entertainment: Classic Vegas

Chapter 7
Back In The 'Bad' Old Days

Chapter 8
The Sporting Life

Chapter 9
Because I Get Asked ... (Or) In My Humble Opinion

Chapter 10
Just For Fun

Foreword
by Robin Leach

There are 40 million people who visit Las Vegas annually — and every one of them has a question.

More than 100,000 love-mates get married in Sin City (which should prove we aren't) each year. And every newlywed has a question.

So does each one of the five million annual conventioneers. Same for the passengers arriving on the 700 daily flights going through McCarran International Airport. And each of the 5,000 new residents each month who decide to relocate and join more than 1.5 million people (including me, in 1999) who made the same decision.

And now, for the first time all in one place, every question gets an answer in this bible of Sin City: the ultimate book of lists. The top 10 in 100 categories all compiled by "No. 1 Man Around Town," Norm Clarke, the distinguished and distinguishable gossip columnist for the Las Vegas Review-Journal, the city's top-read newspaper.

He's kept one eye open on everything and everybody that shakes, sashays and shimmies in Glitter Gulch — including me — since he arrived from Denver in the fall of 1999. And he's asked more questions than anybody to produce this must-have guide to the world's most exciting city.

Norm answers the questions about everything from wild nightlife to fabulous food, from wedding chapels to show business history. It's indispensable if you're one of our visitors. It's invaluable if you live and work in America's fastest growing city. It's priceless whether you've been here five minutes or 50 years. It's everything — and then some — you ever needed to know about the most incredible city on Earth.

Enjoy. Discover. Learn. And if you've got a follow-up question after devouring this dish, no doubt you'll find the answer in Norm's next column, or the next book he will be demanded to write after this one.

Champagne Wishes and Cheers,
Robin Leach

Chapter 1
High Life & Nightlife

Las Vegas had barely caught its breath at the end of the 1990s, from a skyline-altering building boom and a flood of high-end restaurants. Now it's running out of rope — velvet rope — trying to keep up with an unprecedented explosion of new nightclubs and after-hours playgrounds. Remember Rule No. 1: Vegas is not for amateurs.

Bellagio — Start with the majestic lake and its dancing fountain show and Dale Chihuly's glass ceiling in the hotel lobby. Some of the city's most honored restaurants are available at the Bellagio, among them: Michael Mina Bellagio, Picasso, Prime, Le Cirque, Circo or Olives. Take in Cirque du Soleil's *O*, the No. 1 show in town on most critics' list. Shop in the northern retail corridor, the Bellagio's version of Rodeo Drive. Party at the big nightclub Light or the smaller Caramel, both operated by the same New York management. **702-693-7111**

Caesars Palace — Hail the Forum Shops at Caesars, the ultra-themed mall that introduced retail as a new component in the Las Vegas tourism mix. That cylindrical building in front of the property is the Colosseum, home of Celine Dion's show *A New Day* and Elton John's *The Red Piano*. The sprawling Palace offers all types of dining options, including the acclaimed newcomer (and toney with a capital T) Bradley Ogden restaurant in front of Celine's show, and Terraza, where you dine outdoors overlooking the Garden of the Gods' Pool. The best of the rest are inside the Forum mall: Wolfgang Puck's Spago and Chinois; the Palm; Bertolini's; and that haven for homesick New Yorkers, the Stage Deli. **702-731-7110**

Hard Rock Hotel — The center bar, to some, is the center of the party universe and ultimate happy hunting grounds. Surround yourself with minis, low-cuts and high self-esteem. Dinner options include Nobu for the sushi crowd, Simon

Kitchen & Bar, AJ's Steakhouse, Pink Taco and Lucky's, the 24-hour restaurant. Oh yes, there's the famous Hard Rock pool. Everything you've heard about it is true, including the fact that some of the poolside talent is imported from Club Paradise, the strip club across the street; 4455 Paradise Road. **702-693-5000**

Mandalay Bay — The prime attractions are the wave beach by day, and the House of Blues or rumjungle clubs by night. The pinnacle, if you're connected, is a trip to the House of Blues Foundation Room, with its awe-inspiring view of the Strip. Fine dining options include the 3950 restaurant, Aureole, Wolfgang Puck's Lupo, Red Square, China Grill, Red White & Blue and the designer Mexican food at Border Grill. And the hotel (finally) has a hit show with the Broadway smash *Mamma Mia!* **702-632-7777**

MGM Grand Hotel — Start with the newest: the way-upscale Tabu nightclub is an erotic adventure, with its high-tech projected imagery of the female form on bar tops and granite tables. Exotic international models serve cocktails. Check out the igloo-shaped Tantra Room, complete with its own private bar made entirely of ice. The younger set still swarms the larger Studio 54. Restaurant row is a sight for sore eyes and hungry campers. Emeril's is a transplanted New Orleans gem, Pearl is a Chinese treasure and even the most jaded food critics will swoon over Craftsteak. Other newcomers: Shibuya, Diego, and Fiamma. Wolfgang Puck's Bar & Grill is a major upgrade from his pizza cafe and will be a prime location once the new Cirque du Soleil show opens across the casino. **702-891-1111**

New York-New York — A 150-foot Statue of Liberty welcomes you to the 12 towers of New York City, landmarks rising 47 stories and 529 feet (about one-third the actual size of New York City architecture). A replica of the Brooklyn Bridge is 300 feet long and 50-feet high. For the full flavor of Manhattan, there's Gallagher's steakhouse, Greenberg's Deli and Il Forniao. Take in the view from Nine fine Irishmen. Party like a frat boy at Coyote Ugly or catch Cirque du Soleil's sexiest show, *Zumanity*. **702-740-6969**

Palms — Start with Rain and ghostbar, two of the hottest nightclubs in town, add hip restaurants N9NE and Little Buddha, pool parties, movie premieres plus a celebrity-centric marketing plan, and you have the reasons why Palms became so hot so fast. On top of that (literally), there's Alizé, a world-class French restaurant with a glorious penthouse vista. 4321 W. Flamingo Road. **702-942-7777**

Paris Las Vegas — A trip to the top of the half-scale Eiffel Tower is a fun ride even for those who can't afford a stop at the Eiffel Tower restaurant. Le Village Buffet breaks the standard "around the world" format to tour the different regions of France instead. For the best people-watching, try the sidewalk patio dining at the French steakhouse Mon Ami Gabi, Ah Sin, or the balcony views from the new ultra-lounge Risque. **702-947-7000**

Ritz-Carlton Lake Las Vegas — The great get-away. This Mediterranean-style resort on the edge of Lake Las Vegas (17 miles southeast of the Strip) includes a replica of Florence's Pontevecchio Bridge with 64 suites and rooms built into it. The developers fooled Mother Nature by building a white-sand beach in front of a rock garden waterfall. 55 Strada Nathan, Henderson. **702-568-6858**.

The Venetian — Float on an indoor version of Venice's Grand Canal with gondoliers belting out operatic classics. For a break from the high-end shopping, enjoy the strolling opera singers in authentic costumes or watch tourists watch the "living statue." Topnotch Italian chefs serve up the real deal at Zefferino, Valentino and Cannaletto. No Spaghetti-O's. Delmonico is a red-meat lover's nirvana. *Phantom of the Opera* arrives in 2006. **702-414-1000**

 ## HOTTEST NIGHTCLUBS

Coyote Ugly — A spin-off of the 2000 movie of the same name, this themed nightspot at New York-New York packs 'em in using the movie's gimmick of bartop-dancing female mixologists. Formerly Hamilton's, a swank cigar bar that didn't perform up to snuff, the new venture was an instant hit, making Coyote Ugly "per square foot the most successful bar in America," claims hotel president Felix Rappaport. New York-New York. **702-740-6969**

ghostbar — Since Palms opened in November 2001, the ghostbar has been one of the city's most popular party destinations for the celeb crowd. Party outdoors and drink in one of the most intoxicating views in the western world from the "55th floor" (thanks to some creative numbering on the elevator to deal with various cultural superstitions about floor numbering). Palms, 4321 W. Flamingo Road. **702-942-7777**

House of Blues Foundation Room — A favorite of the see-and-be-seen crowd, despite the postage-stamp dance floor, maxed-out volume, and understaffed bar. VIPs love the ornate private rooms where, rumor has it, a server walked in on Kid Rock and Pamela Anderson during an intimate moment. It's the view that lures big weekend turnouts. Private, except on Mondays. Mandalay Bay. **702-632-7777**

Body English — Facing a wave of new competition after dominating the nightclub in the 1990s, the Hard Rock Hotel answered in 2004 with Body English. Formerly known as Baby's, the renovated club is a throwback. "We wanted it to resemble a 1960s British rock star's mansion," said Hard Rock exec Harry Morton. "There's a big move to get ultra-modern. We wanted a throwback" At the christening weekend, members of 'N Sync joined Joey Fatone at his bachelor party in "The Parlor," the VIP room off the dance floor. Sexiest hookup: The $250,000 Baccarat chandelier has revolving disco ball attached to it. For serious high rollers, there's the $1,000 martini, with a diamond-and-ruby-topped swizzle stick. Hard Rock Hotel. Open Friday through Sunday from 11 p.m. to 4 a.m. 4455 Paradise Road. **702-693-5000**

Light — For the first three years of the Bellagio's existence, nightlife was limited to the Fontana Room and Allegra Lounge, where dancing wasn't encouraged. Then someone saw the Light, the hot New York club. New York operators Andrew Sasson (of Jet bar fame) and Chris Barish brought Big Apple prices: Bottles average about $300 to $330, not counting tax and gratuity; Johnny Walker Blue runs about $700, a magnum of Cristal

$1,600 and Louis XIII $13,000. Not that those bloated prices have dimmed the allure of the nightclub. It's smoking hot and loaded with the celeb crowd. Michael Jordan has been in a number of times. But remember the dress code. Shaquille O'Neal got rejected. Not exactly your tank-top-and-glow-stick crowd. Bellagio. **702-693-8300**

Tabu Ultra Lounge — Ultra, as in maxed out in every possible way, especially the imagery that's projected on the bar tops and huge granite tables which are fortified for dancing. The MGM Grand unveiled this cozier, teched-up counterpart to sister club Studio 54 as a means to keep the well-heeled crowd (read: money) from checking out off-property options. Now they're checking out Tabu's talk-of-the-town model servers. MGM Grand. **702-891-1111**

Ra — According to Ra's British publicist, Mark Jay, Las Vegas is becoming recognized in Europe as the "party-scene equivalent of Ibiza." This heavily-themed blend of Egyptian and futuristic elements has been aggressive in marketing itself as ground zero for the Euro crowd. Top Brit deejays are regulars. Luxor. **702-632-7777**

Rain Nightclub — Rain never had a sprinkling of celebrities; it was a deluge from Day One. It might be the most contemporary dance/concert venue in the United States, when more than 4,000 revelers pass through the silver-metallic tunnel entry on the busiest nights. At 25,000 square foot, Rain holds about 1,800 revelers at a time. VIP skyboxes go for up to $1,000 plus a two-bottle minimum (Bottles start at $275). A "water wall" cools down the three-foot fireballs that erupt over the elevated dance area. Eight "water booths" offer liquid-filled leather banquettes. On New Year's Eve 2003, Britney Spears and friends partied in one skybox; Kobe and Vanessa Bryant watched from another. Palms, 4321 W. Flamingo Road. **702-938-9999**

rumjungle — Dine, then dance to dueling congas amid walls of fire and water in this Brazilian-themed supper club. A meat-eater's extravaganza. My recommendation: "The Chocolate Cake." Bite into a sugar coated wedge of lemon, count to three and knock back a shot of Frangelica. The restaurant tables are cleared for dancing and nightclub action at 11 p.m. Mandalay Bay. **702-632-7408**

Studio 54 — Ricky Martin shook his bon bon here and hardly anyone noticed. He went unrecognized in his baseball cap-and-sunglasses disguise after the 2000 Billboard Music Awards. This upscale, 22,000-square-foot version of the New York legend licensed the name and appropriated the original Studio 54 moon to hang over the dance floor. There's a very cool collection of VIP photographs from the Warhol era. The non-stop action includes an aerialist show, smoke machines and confetti cannons. The re-launch of *Dance Fever* was shot here in the summer of 2003. MGM Grand Hotel. **702-891-1111**

 THE AFTER HOURS CROWD

Las Vegas always has been an all-night party. In the old days, the post-midnight action was centered around "Midnight Idol" Wayne Newton crooning a 12:30 a.m. show, or Louis Prima in the Casbar lounge. Today's night owls tend to entertain themselves, often

in restaurants that have discovered how to keep the drinks (and revenue) flowing long after the dinner hour.

Alesium Afterhours — Seven nightclub opened in August 2001 after a hip makeover of the failed Country Star themed restaurant. Orange County nightclub operator Tony Verdugno, who created Drai's Afterhours, left Drai's to open Alesium Afterhours and took a lot of the crowd with him. The insanity begins at 2 a.m. 3724 S. Las Vegas Blvd. **702-739-7744**

Drai's Afterdark — Still the center of Sin City's after-hours universe. Victor Drai's upscale see-and-be-seen club rages from about 3 a.m. until mid-morning. Drai, a former Hollywood producer, was once married to actress Kelly LeBrock and lived with Jacqueline Bisset. I've seen lines of 200-plus snaking through the Barbary Coast casino at midnight on weekends. Barbary Coast. **702-737-7111**

Dragon — The '60s-cool lounge of the China Grill restaurant at Mandalay Bay converts to an after-hours club at 11 p.m. on Wednesdays. Mandalay Bay. **702-632-7777**

Ice — Formerly the Drink and Eat Too, this revamped off-Strip newcomer stays open until 7 a.m. on Saturday nights. 200 East Harmon Ave. **702-699-9888**

Light — On celeb-heavy weekends, Light lands more than its share of Hollywood bold-faced names, high rollers, and the women who love them. You gotta pay to play here; at $25, Light has the most expensive cover in town. Bellagio. **702-693-8300**

OPM — The after-hours action starts at 3 a.m. on the second floor of Wolfgang Puck's Chinois at the Forum Shops at Caesars. Ashanti and Jessica Simpson attended the opening night party and R. Kelly had an after-concert party here. Caesars Palace. **702-369-4998**

Tabu Ultra Lounge — If I had just 24 hours to spend in Sin City, too many of them would be spent here. The MGM Grand's all-out addition to the nightlife scene takes luxe to a new level. Tabu's white-hot models/servers are as much a draw as the interactive imagery; move a drink and a "flame" shoots across the granite table. *Time* magazine had Tabu on their cover of its 2004 Las Vegas spread. When he's in town, Tom Jones has been seen rating the talent in the VIP room. Last call is at 7 a.m. every morning. MGM Grand Hotel. **702-891-1111**

Risqué — A view James Bond would kill for. Paris Las Vegas joined the exploding "lounge" trend in early 2003, building this room at the same time as the new Ah Sin Asian restaurant downstairs. Six balconies overlook the Strip and the Bellagio's dancing fountains. Risqué bills itself as the city's only drinks-and-dessert club. Paris Las Vegas. **702-946-7000**

rumjungle — Remember, the rum drinks sneak up on you; two Volcanoes and you'll be speaking an untranslatable furry-tongued dialect. Ask Woody Harrelson. During the 1999 filming of *Play It to the Bone* with Antonio Banderas, Harrelson was seen being carried out the door by friends after learning the hard way: It's a (rum)jungle out there. The Volcanoes erupt until 5 a.m. on weekends. Mandalay Bay. **702-632-7777**

Studio 54 — Party like it's 1979. The launch of Dollhouse Thursdays pushed the erotica envelope at an already popular club. The concept is simple. For a price, male and female models will change into whatever sexy look VIP patrons prefer: sultry nurse, cheerleading vixen, or hunky male stripper in bare-chested tuxedo and short-shorts. MGM Grand. **702-891-1111**

 EVERY NIGHT'S A PARTY

Of course it is. That's why you come to Las Vegas. But people live here too, so each club tends to pick one night when it goes the extra mile or adds an unusual twist for locals. Here's an exercise to show you really can find a party here seven nights a week . . .

Sunday — The House of Blues at Mandalay Bay hosts Sin Sundays, a party catering to the service industry, featuring world-class deejays and themed events. The Bellagio's Light club also has Social Night, another service-industry night, with no cover charge.

Monday — The House of Blues Foundation Room is open to the public on Mondays. Few things in Las Vegas are more impressive than the view from the open-air patio. Also, The Beach nightclub has bar and restaurant employees night, with $600 cash prizes for the hottest babes.

Tuesday — The MGM Grand's Studio 54 club is the home of the highly popular EDEN (Erotically Delicious Entertainers Night), which brings out the top dancers in local entertainment.

In warmer months, Palm's pool venue, Skin, dedicates Tuesdays to an event quaintly known as Skinny Dip. It's billed as the city's biggest outdoor party, drawing as many as 3,000 revelers. Play outdoor blackjack among fog machines, mermaids and go-go dancers. Other Palms visitors head upstairs to ghostbar for hip-hop night.

Wednesday — Ladies are free at the Luxor's Ra club, while next door at Mandalay Bay the China Grill's lounge begins its transformation into Dragon, turning into a loungy, club-crowd scene at 11 p.m.

Thursday — Bikinis at the Rio has free drinks for local ladies until midnight. At the same casino's Club Rio, it's Latin Libido Night and you never know who you might see; Ben Affleck and Jennifer Lopez showed up one night.

Friday — Sedona, a locals happy-hour scene way west of the Strip (9580 W. Flamingo Road) offers a sexy vibe that made it one of the instant hits of 2003. The House of Blues' Flashback Fridays feature the best of '80s pop, rock and new wave dance music. Nostalgia for the Billy Idol years seems to attract large groups of women and bachelorette parties.

Saturday — The House of Blues takes another time trip, via the Boogie Knights, a tongue-in-cheek disco band with cheesy wigs and a huge following.

Robin Leach's ten picks to indulge the best champagne and caviar lifestyle in Las Vegas, whether you bring a date or are looking for one.

Start with the hair by checking in with stylist-to-the-stars Michael Boychuck at either the Canyon Ranch Salon in the Venetian or the AMP Salon at Palms.

To look your finest for a night on the town, check in at D. Fine inside The Mirage, or Pal Zeiri and Lior in the Venetian's Grand Canal retail area.

Fire up the evening's mood at the Venetian's V Bar or Spago in the Forum Shops at Caesars. There's always a posse of PYT's (Pretty Young Things) to raise the spirits.

For delightful, decadent dinners, choose between superstar chefs: Wolfgang Puck's Postrio at the Venetian or Chef Jean-Georges Vongerichten's Prime at the Bellagio.

For high-style romance and seductive dining, choose between Alex Stratta's Renoir at The Mirage, Andre Rochat's Alizé at Palms or something a little more casual at Kirk Oderlie's off-Strip Jazzed Cafe.

If it's a hip dining spot you seek, choose between steaks at Simon Kitchen & Bar in the Hard Rock Hotel or N9NE Steakhouse at Palms, or between sushi at Nobu in the Hard Rock or Little Buddha at Palms.

Late-night shows turn up the temperature. I'd recoazy Girls at the Riviera. But if you're going out earlier, the pure entertainment value lies with Clint Holmes at Harrah's or the Scintas at the Rio. For an elaborate production, see Cirque du Soleil's *Mystère* at Treasure Island or *O* at Bellagio.

ghostbar at the top of Palms, offers an incredible view and an abundance of fun-loving, beautiful people. If you want it wilder on the dance floor, then splash down to the ground-level Rain nightclub.

For the best champagne and caviar, flash a smile and a platinum card in Julian Serrano's Picasso at the Bellagio, Napoleon's lounge at Paris Las Vegas, David Feau's Lutèce at The Venetian or Charlie Palmer's amazing Aureole at Mandalay Bay.

For bedroom eyes and primal passion, check into the finest high roller suites. It takes a roll of the dice to choose between those at the Venetian, Caesars Palace, MGM Grand and Bellagio. But don't forget those suites with the stripper poles at Palms!

 ## "LOCALS" HANGOUTS

Yes, there is a Las Vegas beyond the Strip. Here are some good reasons to find it should the crowds and intensity of Las Vegas Boulevard start to wear you down.

The Bootlegger — This might be the most happening place in the whole country that's owned by a politician with a bootlegger in the family. Lt. Gov. Lorraine Hunt and her family operate this Old Vegas hotspot. When Frank Sinatra pal Sonny King isn't singing up a storm, the drop-ins include the likes of Robert Goulet, Clint Holmes and the Scintas. Hugh Hefner had heads spinning when he marched in with his bevy of blondes for a birthday party in 2001. Among the awestruck: local Roman Catholic priests emeritus Caesar Caviglia and John McVeigh. "We're going over to hear confessions," Caviglia whispered to our table in a conspiratorial tone. "The bishop won't believe this." Monday night's karaoke with Kelly Clinton brings in a fun bunch often instigated by Holmes. 7700 Las. Vegas Blvd. South. **702-736-4939**

Crown & Anchor Pub — The preferred gathering spot of Brits and locals who love the pub scene and traditional English fare. "It's like 'Cheers.' You never feel too old to go there," says one local PR type. There is often live music, and Thursday is "Trivia Night." As far as the menu, start with the assumption that everything is a heart attack on a plate, so diet be damned and full speed ahead. 1350 E. Tropicana Ave. **702-739-0281**

Double Down Saloon — *Stuff* magazine added to the Double Down's growing rep by naming it one of the nation's top 20 dives in January 2003, the only Nevada watering hole so honored. The article included a photo that pretty much captured the Double Down's flavor: a topless customer riding a coin-operated supermarket horse with the bumper sticker on it that read: "Ride it like you stole it." Owner P. Moss told me, "Her name is Star. It's her real name," he added, leaving the impression that assumed names are not a rarity among his clientele. The Double Down started off 10 years ago "as just another dive bar, and now it's a very well known dive bar," said Moss. In late 2002, the hotspot was named "bar of the month" on Playboy.com. Then Comedy Central host Dave Atell took Double Double's rep national with a visitation of his show *Insomniac*. 4640 Paradise Road. **702-791-5775**

Fellini's Italian Dining — Owner Bob Harry turned this one-time Shakey's Pizza into a cozy, dark Italian restaurant that's a magnet for diners who want a side order of entertainment. Much like the Bootlegger, you never know who's going to show up at the piano bar. One night in January 2002 it was '50's teen idol Frankie Avalon, recounting his early years at the Sands.

Engelbert Humperdinck, Steve Lawrence and Al Martino also have stopped in to take a turn at the mic or grab dinner. 5555 W. Charleston Blvd. **702-870 -9999**

Gordon Biersch Brewing Company — One of the most popular singles spots in town brews its beer on-site and serves it with upscale pub food. Its location in the Hughes Center office park also makes it one of the few "white collar" hangouts in a blue-collar town. 3987 Paradise Road. **702-312-5247**

J.C. Wooloughan — Tucked inside the discreet J.W. Marriott hotel in suburban Summerlin is a pub that really rocks, with butt-kicking Celtic bands and authentic Irish fare contributing to an authentic atmosphere. It's Party Central on St. Patrick's Day. 221 N. Rampart Blvd. **702-869-7777**

Piero's Italian Cuisine — A historic gathering point for the classic Vegas power crowd and still a place to spot Sinatra's kind of dames. 355 Convention Center Drive. **702-369-2305**.

Roadrunner Saloon — This local franchise reminds me of the upscale sports bars in Denver where hundreds of Bronco fans gathered on Sundays to watch the game and make new friends. It's so comfortable that 60 cast members of *Mystere* had a going-away party at the new West Flamingo location on a Sunday night. This comment nailed it: "It's like a high school reunion; but a good high school reunion." 2430 E. Pebble Road, Henderson. **702-948-8282**; 9820 W. Flamingo Road, **702-243-5329**; 2839 W. Sahara Ave., **702-227-8787**; 921 N. Buffalo Drive. **702-242-2822**

Sand Dollar Blues Lounge — Hang around this biker bar long enough and you'll see a lot of big names drop in for a jam session. Huey Lewis and his sax player Rob Suddeth joined Mark Hummel's house band during the 2003 Labor Day weekend. With the fans shouting for "The Heart of Rock and Roll," Lewis played three tunes on his harmonica and sang to an ecstatic crowd. Blind guitar virtuoso Jeff Healey walked in one day with his band and, one by one, each band member joined the house band, the Moanin' Black Snakes, for a half dozen songs. On another occasion, rock legend Dave Mason, who wrote "We Just Disagree," joined the fun. 3355 W. Spring Mountain Road. **702-871-6651**

Sedona — After Adam Corrigan and his brothers turned the Roadrunner Saloons into locals' favorites, he wanted to try his hand at something else. Backed by Andre Agassi, the tennis great's longtime manager Perry Rogers, and new Golden Nugget co-owner Tom Breiting, Corrigan came up with another winner. Classy and seductive, it's the hottest thing on the west side of town. "A ghostbar for locals," said Angela Sampras, co-producer of the X show. It's open 24 hours and gets a strong late crowd. 9580 W. Flamingo Road. **702-320-4700**

TOP SPAS

Aquae Sulis Spa — Venture far from the Strip to find the place voted Las Vegas' best spa by the *Wall Street Journal* in 2001. Signature features: aura reading therapy, hot-stone massage, margarita-flavored salt scrub, and multi-colored mud treatments. J.W. Marriott, 221 N. Rampart Blvd. **702-869-7807**

Canyon Ranch Spa Club — This cavernous 65,000-square-foot facility offers a vast array of massage options and services. The royal treatment: the Rasul Ritual and the Lulur King's Bath are billed as "supremely indulgent experiences." The Venetian. **702-414-3600**

The Four Seasons Spa — Signature services include champagne mud wraps, French body polishes, therapeutic baths and seaweed body masks. The Swedish and therapeutic are the most popular massages. The Zen Garden massage involves warms rocks while Jamu is described as almost spiritual, with various scented oils. The spa is limited to hotel guests only, but said guests can call for "room service" and have two tables set up in a hotel room. Four Seasons. **702-632-5302**

MGM Grand Spa — Milk-and-honey body wraps are a specialty in this full-service spa. Exfoliating treatments and a variety of facial options are popular, too. MGM Grand Hotel. **702-891-3077**

Oasis Spa — The only 24-hour spa on the Strip means there is no reason not to have a Swedish massage at 5 a.m. Popular services include the river stone massage, aromatherapy and deep-tissue sports massage, reflexology, body wraps, sea-salt scrub glows and refresher facials. Luxor. **702-730-5724**

Spa Vita di Lago — A 30,000-square-foot complex offers a separate swimming pool, a meditation garden, full-service beauty salon, Vichy showers, a fitness center and speciality spa services. Resort guests are not required to pay an entry fee to the spa. Ritz-Carlton Lake Las Vegas, 55 Strada Nathan, Henderson. **702-567-4700**

Spa Bellagio — A Europe-in-Vegas experience, with a full range of massages, facials and body and salon treatments. Massages range from a 25-minute Swedish session for $55 to the 50-minute, in-room version for $190. Couples can try the in-room tandem massage with two trained therapists at 70 minutes for $175. The spa is moving to the Bellagio's new tower in late 2004. Bellagio. **702-693-7472**.

Spa Mandalay — The August 2001 issue of *Muscle & Fitness* gave Spa Mandalay its highest rating, calling it "the lushest and most beautiful of any spa on the Strip" and giving it a 5-star "Pampering Quotient." The 30,000-square-foot facility features tandem massages, a eucalyptus body wrap, a number of Ayurvedic treatments and volcanic dust masks. The facility also features steam rooms, saunas, whirlpools and cold plunges. Mandalay Bay. **702-632-7777**

The Spa at Caesars Palace — The art of indulgence, Roman-style. Private men's and women's VIP massage suites and lounges. Services include body wraps, sea-salt treatments, Ayurvedic rituals and exotic Hawaiian, Japanese and Balinese therapies. There is also a 6,500-square-foot fitness facility featuring virtual reality stair-steppers, a rock-climbing wall and a yoga studio. The spa is open to the public Sundays through Thursdays, but restricted to hotel guests Fridays and Saturdays. Caesars Palace. **702-731-7776**

Dolphin Court Salon & Day Spa — The Green Valley Ranch location gets high marks and recommendations from many locals and several celebrities, such as Joan Severance and Robin Leach. Green Valley Ranch, 2300 Paseo Verde Parkway, **702-992-9000**. Other locations: 3455 S. Durango Blvd., **702-949-9999**; and 7581 W. Lake Mead Blvd., **702-946-6000**.

 ## TOP 10 HOTEL POOLS

Bellagio — Off the charts in every detail. The symmetrical design of the five pools captures Old World splendor in the classical setting of a Mediterranean villa. The lush layout features Italian cypresses, olive and citrus trees, climbing vines and five kinds of roses. You can rent a cabana for $150 weekdays, $200 weekends. Bellagio. **702-693-7111**

Caesars Palace — The new Greco-Roman pool is opulent to the maximus, serving as a Heidi Klum location shoot for *Sports Illustrated's* 2001 swimsuit issue. Caesars' design was inspired by the ancient Baths of Caracalla, a tourist attraction near Rome. The cabana-enclosed Venus pool was the first "European-style" (i.e. topless) one in town, an innovation copied by Mandalay Bay in the summer of 2003. Caesars Palace. **702-731-7110**

Whiskey Beach — This layout is aces as it seems to flow for miles just out the backdoor of the Whiskey Bar at Green Valley Ranch. The lavishly landscaped eight-acre site offers a view of the Strip about 10 miles away. The 13 private cabanas include TVs, telephone, ceiling fans, misting systems, sofas and changing rooms, as well as access to the private lap pools located directly in front of their sandy beach front. There is an adjacent outdoor cafe and amphitheater for concerts and special events. Green Valley Ranch, 2300 Paseo Verde Parkway, Henderson. **702-617-7777**

Hard Rock Hotel — Pamela Anderson, among many other bikini-clad (and some unclad) hotties, promoted this as one of the most popular pool scenes after the Hard Rock opened in 1995. Later hotels copied some of the ideas, such as cabanas, an underwater sound system, a lazy river, water slide, hot tubs and two sandy beach areas. There's a swim-up blackjack area and the Palapa Hut with four blackjack tables. Hard Rock Hotel, 4455 Paradise Road. **702-693-5000**

Flamingo — A palm-dotted tropical oasis covers five acres with tiered lagoon pools, waterfalls and a wildlife habitat with exotic birds and decorative fish. It's perhaps the best-kept pool secret on the Strip, and one of the few the public can access without being a hotel guest. If there was a Top 10 for romantic-evening strolls, this would be among the top two, right up there with the Ritz-Carlton's lakeside pathway. Flamingo. **702-733-3111**

Mandalay Bay — The premier beach layout in town. The wave-pool area takes up most of the 11 acres, but there's also a lazy river winding past palm trees and cabanas. Brad Pitt and Julia Roberts had separate wrap parties here for *The Mexican*, with Roberts successfully negotiating bigger waves than her co-star. The much buzzed-about Moorea Beach Club, a European-style (topless) tanning venue, opened next to the wave pool in the fall of 2003. On weekends it becomes an ultra lounge at 10 p.m. Mandalay Bay. **702-632-7777**

MGM Grand Hotel — The 27,000-square-foot Grand Pool complex includes a flowing 1,000-foot-long river pool, the city's longest ride of its kind. The area is one of the largest anywhere, accommodating 2,500 people. MGM Grand Hotel. **702-891-1111**

Palms — What it lacks in size, the venue known as Skin makes up for with its intimacy and hipness quotient. Britney Spears sunbathed here in her red bikini before a night on the town with Palms' Maloof brothers, George and Phil, in April 2003. Palms, 4321 W. Flamingo Road. **702-942-7777**

Paris Las Vegas — An A-plus setting. Imagine a third-floor pool in the shadow of the model Eiffel Tower, with a view of the Bellagio's lake across the street. Now picture the hotel's hot-air balloon marquee in the skyline and one of Nevada's fiery sunsets. Paris Las Vegas. **702-946-7000**

Ritz-Carlton Lake Las Vegas — It's smaller than the others, but offers a white-sand beach and scores additional points for the pristine, private setting next to Lake Las Vegas and that stirring view of the Pontevecchio Bridge. 55 Strada Nathan, Henderson. **702-568-6858**

TOP SALONS

Amp — Michael Boychuck, who trained with Hollywood stylist of the stars Jose Eber, runs a fun ship. The premier hair colorist was dubbed "The Blonde Maker" by Joan Van Ark because of a long list of blonde clientele, including Kirsten Dunst, Paris Hilton, Donna D' Errico ("Baywatch"), Jenny McCarthy, Josie Bisset, and Jenny Garth. Boychuck came to Las Vegas in 1998, and opened Amp in November 2001 after working at the Bellagio and Venetian."Amp has a fun, New York sort of feel," says Joan Severance, two-time *Playboy* cover girl. "Michael Boychuck, the best colorist in the west, tends to my now-blonde tresses with utmost flair." An Amp afficionado: "I like it because it's such a social scene; everyone's talking. Some places have private areas for everything, the pedicures, manicures. At Amp, everything's right there. It's perfect for some good old-fashioned salon gossip." Palms, 4321 W. Flamingo Road. **702-942-6909**

Bellagio — When Steve Wynn opened Bellagio in 1998, he brought in Los Angeles celebrity stylist Laurent Prive as a partner and introduced him as "the best in the world." A year later, in an industry shocker, Prive was out, told only that it was "a business decision." Insiders hint Wynn misjudged the revenue projections and wasn't willing to allow Prive's whopping profits. During the filming of the *Ocean's Eleven* remake, I'm told Andy Garcia was the only cast member who showed up at the salon, rather than getting the VIP treatment in the high-roller villas. Bellagio. **702-693-8080**

Canyon Ranch — After a slow start when The Venetian opened in 1999, the spa hired Michael Boychuck as salon director in late 2000. Kerastace, the high-end product line from Loreal, ranks Canyon Ranch among the top five salons in the country for its accounts. Revenues were near $4 million in 2003. Canyon Ranch had a staff of 50-plus even before the Venetian's 1,000-room expansion in mid-2003. Clients have included Paris Hilton, Kirsten Dunst, Rick Springfield, Susan Anton, the Riviera's Crazy Girls and other Las Vegas headliners, not to mention five local news anchors. The Venetian. **702-414-3606**

Diva Studio — Owner Steven Brooks was "born and raised" in the salon business, he says. His father was a hair dresser for Vidal Sasson and Paul Mitchell in Los Angeles. After moving to Las Vegas, Brooks hooked up with his future wife, hair stylist Lisa Shriver, and they opened Diva Studio in 1993 with $25,000 of their savings (they "couldn't even get a loan"). "We are an employee-based operation; everybody works as an employee, not as an independent contractor," Brooks says. The full-service branch of the operation has included the wedding of baseball slugger Mark McGwire and a "Miss *Playboy* Search." Clients include Cindy Crawford and No Doubt singer Gwen Stefani. One location; 8876 S. Eastern Ave. **702-933-3482**

Dolphin Court Salon — It's part of the Dolphin Court Spa, which overlooks the Whiskey Beach courtyard at Green Valley Ranch. Five manicure and five pedicure stations offer hot stone, peppermint and green-tea-leaf treatment. Green Valley Ranch, 2300 Paseo Verde Parkway, Henderson. **702-617-7777**

Paris — As her name suggests, beauty services director Jean Starr has worked with many top celebs over two decades in Las Vegas. She oversees eight hair stations, three spa pedicure chairs, seven manicure stations and eight aesthetics rooms for waxing and facials. A licensed cosmetologist serves as makeup artist for many brides who marry in the Paris chapel. Paris Las Vegas. **702-946-7000**

Ritz-Carlton — This early 2003 arrival has a balcony overlooking Lake Las Vegas, not to mention seven hair stations, four manicure stations and four pedicure stations with massaging chairs. 55 Strada Nathan, Henderson. **702-568-6858**

Robert Cromean Salon — Cromean, who bases operations in San Diego, is rated by many as the top in his field of education and platform work, and a trend-setter in styling techniques. "He's got a great name," said a competitor. "He's one of those who you want to know what he's doing, a real innovator on the educational side. He sets the standards in his area of expertise." Mandalay Bay. **702-632-7777**

Square — After opening in 1995 with so-so success, "I was thinking about getting out. Then the (Las Vegas) boom hit and I decided to stay," said Rob Hollis, who operates Square with his wife Patricia Hood. "We were five stylists and now we're over 30." The boom helped, but so did Square's spirit of volunteerism. "The things that helped us the most was doing charity events and special events, helping the community, advertising through those avenues.""He's a local leader," Amp's Boychuck says of Hollis. Square has been hired to do the *Billboard Music Awards* here for six years. Notable clients include the cast of *That '70s Show* and comedian Louie Anderson ("He was like the John Gotti of comedy; wanted his hair cut every night," Hollis says). 231 N. Buffalo Drive. **702-255-7050**

William Whatley International Salon — Things are rockin' for Colorado native William Whatley. The stylist met 'N Sync during a Las Vegas tour stop and they signed on as sponsors of his hair care line. Shirley MacLaine also stops in. Comedian Kay Cannon of *The Second City* comedy troupe is another convert: "William, or as *The Second City* calls him, 'Sir William, Duke of Hair,' is unlike any hairstylist I know. His infectious energy and cackling laughter resonate throughout the salon," she says. 7985 W. Sahara Ave. **702-256-8669**

 HEY BIG SPENDER

In a city built on the foundation of making customers happy, especially the high roller, excess is inevitable. Sin City isn't all about sex; it's about making an art form out of living large.

PRIME — The most expensive drink in town? A shot of 50-year-old scotch at Bellagio's Prime restaurant will cost you $1,050, which edges out the $1,000 martini at Body English, the Hard Rock Hotel's new nightclub. In late 2003, Prime steak house landed a bottle of Chivas Royal Salute, one of 255 bottles tapped from the Coronation Cask celebrating the Queen's Golden Jubilee and sold to private buyers. At $10,000 a bottle, 10 were shipped to the U.S., where a Brinks security truck met the shipment. "We're the only place on the planet where you can actually have a shot," said Prime general manager Roy Saunders. The joke at Prime is "You can drink over $1,000 worth of liquor and still drive legally." High rollers who tried it said it was "phenomenally smooth," said Saunders. Bellagio. **702-693-7223**

Le Cirque — The house record for a check here is $75,000. Along with dinner, the party of 15 put away two bottles of 1961 Chateau Petrus ($17,295 each), two bottles of 1947 Chateau Cheval Blanc ($12,535), various champagnes and finished with $600 shots of Hardy's Perfection. Bellagio. **702-693-7223**

The Seafood Tower at Osteria del Circo — Forty pounds of mouth-watering decadence: six Maine lobster tails, a dozen stone crab claws, two dozen oysters, a dozen jumbo shrimp, amachi and ahi tuna tartare, all stacked more than three feet high on a giant sea scallop-like shell and topped with beluga caviar. Yours for a mere $1,200. Serves six. Bellagio. **702-693-7223**

MGM Grand Hotel Mansion — This separate building tucked behind the emerald-green behemoth is an ultra-private haven once available only to the highest of high-rollers. It's now open to the public, at least those members of the public who can afford an average nightly rate of $7,000. Deposit fee: Your first born. MGM Grand Hotel. **702-891-1111**

Palms' Real World *suite* — You can camp out in the *Real World* suite, home of the over-sexed cast of the MTV hit show, for $5,000 a night during the week or $7,500 on the weekend. But Palms owner George Maloof is justifiably fussy about who stays there. If your name is Britney Spears, no problem. She reportedly serenaded him for a couple hours after a night on the town in late March 2003. The view from this suite reportedly inspired the sudden marriage between Spears and homeboy pal Jason Alexander on January 3, 2004. Palms, 4321 W. Flamingo Road. **702-942-7777**

Picasso — The price of wine at the Bellagio gourmet room would pay off a lot of mortgages. There's a 1945 Chateau Mouton Rothschild for $16,888; 1947 Chateau Cheval Blanc, $15,610; and a 1961 Chateau Petrus Classic, $13,500. After dinner, perhaps you'd fancy a Hardy Perfection cognac at $625 a shot? "We had a group of Russian people in one night and a guy bought 11 shots," said chef Julian Serrano. Then there's the Foie Gras Guy who devoured six orders of the artery-clogging appetizer at $22 a pop. Bellagio. **702-693-7223**

The Ritz-Carlton's Valentine Special — Three nights in the Presidential Suite (normally $5,000 a night), a personal butler, his-and-hers Bulgari watches, a new Mercedes SLK convertible to take home, unlimited golf and spa use, a VIP invitation to the star-studded "Diamonds & The Power of Love" exhibit and breakfast in bed. All this for just $95,000 in a special promotion celebrating the hotel's opening in 2003. And, yes, they had a taker and have made the special an annual tradition. 55 Strada Nathan, Henderson. **702-568-6858**

Shintaro — One look at the menu will tell you Shintaro's target diners are the Asian high rollers. How else do you explain $40 for a free range chicken, $75 for prime New York sirloin, and Kobe steaks ranging from the $190 tenderloin (10 ounces) to the $200 rib eye (14 ounces). Don't even think of the c-word (catsup). Bellagio. **702-693-7111**

Valentino — The Italian definition of decadence: paper-thin slices of aged parmigiano reggiano, drizzled with white truffle-flavored honey. "We call it food for the gods," says Chef Luciano Pellegrini who won the James Beard Best Chef of the Southwest award in 2004. You won't find it on the menu, but you sure will impress people by asking for it. The Venetian. **702-414-1000**

London Club — The restaurant has closed but the story is so over-the-top Vegas it must be included. Bird's nest soup at the Aladdin's short-lived London Club went for $125 a bowl. "The bird nest (ingredients) comes from caves in China," explained chef Jacques Von Staden, now at Andre Rochat's Alizé . "The nests are held together by bird spittle, which Asians consider an aphrodisiac. We pay $1,700 a pound for it and charge $150 an ounce. I've seen patrons request up to five, six ounces in the broth." And these were 2000 prices!

GAY CLUBS AND BARS

Backstreet — There's always a party somewhere in Las Vegas, and this club draws big crowds on Sunday, both in the afternoons and evenings. Country dancing is the beacon, and the crowd runs the gamut from rough-tough cowboy to milk maids. 5012 S. Arville Road. **702-876-1844**

Buffalo — Leather is in year-round here, and so are cheap drinks and nice bartenders. You will see lots of daddies (older men) and bears (teddy-bear body types). 4640 Paradise Road. **702-733-8355**

Las Vegas Eagle — Wednesdays and Fridays mean free beer busts to guys who get down to their underwear. 3430 E. Tropicana Ave.. **702-458-8662**

Freezone — It bills itself as the largest gay restaurant in Las Vegas, with accommodations for weddings, birthdays, and special events. Fridays and Saturdays feature the cabaret female-impersonator show *What a Drag*. 610 Naples Drive. **702-794-2300**

Gipsy — It's the biggest and busiest of Las Vegas alternative clubs, voted three times as Las Vegas' Best Gay Nightclub in the *Las Vegas Review-Journal's* annual Best of Las Vegas readers' poll. 4605 South Paradise Road. **702-731-1919**

Goodtimes – Mondays are a big night here. The party runs from midnight until 6 a.m. at a club which shares the same strip mall as the Liberace Museum. 1775 E. Tropicana Ave. **702-736-9494**

Hamburger Mary's — This restaurant and bar chain features Thursdays as '80s night with deejay Dusty Street, a West Coast deejay legend. 4503 S. Paradise Road. **702-735-4400**

Icon — The women's club formerly known as Angles is now under new ownership and re-establishing itself. 4633 Paradise Road. **702-791-0100**

Sasha's Restaurant & Bar — Drag club with shows every night, including under-21 events (no alcohol). Mondays feature a cabaret showcase and Tuesdays are Lesbians Entertainment Night. Bartender Joey is a legend; he was named the top bartender in town in a citywide contest a few years back. 4640 Paradise Road. **702-735-3888**

Snicks Place — This downtown locals hangout leans toward the seedy side but stays busy. 1402 S. 3rd St., **385-9298**

TOP ALTERNATIVE EVENTS
(where gays and straights meet)

Courtesy of Joshua Ryan, AKA Sasha Scarlett, co-owner of Sasha's Restaurant and Bar, 4640 Paradise Road. Joshua has been voted one of America's Top 10 Drag Queens by the E! cable network. He has been married for 22 years and is "the proud father of three amazingly well-adjusted children."

Las Vegas Pride — Clint Holmes, Susan Anton, Alexandra Paul (*Baywatch*), and Paige O'Hara (voice of Belle in *Beauty and the Beast*) are among the straight performers who have turned out for Las Vegas Pride, demonstrating their support of diversity in the community. In 2003, the Pride Festival decided to move indoors from its usual park setting, and attracted even more major headliners. **702-678-5600**

Las Vegas Fetish and Fantasy Halloween Ball — More than 4,000 people have celebrated their fantasies at this raucous, fun soiree, which features everything from adult video stars to snake charmers and fire breathers. The event was voted "One of the Top 10 Parties in the World" by the Travel Channel.

Nevada's Bighorn Rodeo — One of 28 gay rodeo events in the International Gay Rodeo circuit, the Bighorn draws thousands and helps raise money for AIDS-related charities in the community. "Gay rodeo" may sound like an oxymoron until you see the bulls, barrel racing and bronc busting. This is a real rodeo.

Pimp and Ho Ball — This Halloween party has grown large enough to stage in arenas, most recently the Orleans Arena. Stars such as Tommy Lee blend in with a well-dressed, wild and sexy club crowd in a gathering that brings the beautiful people together to rock the night away.

AIDSWalk — This annual event brings in thousands of walkers to help raise money for the fight against AIDS. The event also raises community awareness and has garnered deep corporate support.

Golden Rainbow's "Ribbon of Life" — "Showkids" from revues along the Strip step out to display their versatility by recreating numbers from Broadway musicals. Local headliners such as Sheena Easton and Charo also lend their talents to the largest AIDS fundraiser in Nevada.

National Coming-Out Day Festivities — The *Las Vegas Bugle* newspaper teams with local gay bars to create an event in the "Fruit Loop" — the area where Swenson Street and Paradise Road meet near the Hard Rock Hotel — to celebrate "coming out" in Las Vegas. It has drawn more than 3,000 people and benefited the Center of Southern Nevada (formerly the Gay and Lesbian Center).

Burning Man Festival — This one is located 8 hours north of Las Vegas in the desert outside of Fallon, Nevada, but you still can't leave it off the list. Burning Man brings together artists, poets, hippies and weirdos for a week-long celebration that now attracts more than 30,000 people each year.

Black & White Ball — The AFAN (Aid for AIDS of Nevada) Food Pantry feeds thousands who struggle for basic necessities. This benefit crosses gay and straight boundaries as a social event, featuring national entertainers such as Taylor Dayne.

New Year's Eve — Organizers of the successful Pride Festival have created an incredible New Year's Eve event to be held at Spring Valley Manor, 6080 South Jones Blvd. This is an event that attracted more than 500 people and included a spectacular view of the Las Vegas fireworks.

Chapter 2
Celebrity City

My first Las Vegas celebrity sighting? The summer of 1979. Andre's French Restaurant. I was in town on assignment for The Associated Press, talking shop with AP photographer Lenny Ignelzi when I looked to my left and recognized her legs first. No one had sticks like actress/dancer Juliet Prowse. Here's the creme de la creme of Las Vegas sightings, thanks to my legion of spies.

Ben Affleck and **Jennifer Lopez**, taking dance lessons at Club Rio's Latin La-Beat-Oh Night during their 2002 Thanksgiving visit.

James Brown, dressed in a bathrobe, ranting at patrons, throwing a chair and claiming he communicated with the Pope during a bizarre New Year's Eve 2000 performance at the Aladdin's.

A directionally-challenged **Bobby Knight**, rolling down his window at a downtown stoplight and asking local public relations man Ken Rubino how to get to the airport. Knight sightings set off rumors he was in town checking out the University of Nevada, Las Vegas, basketball job in early 2001. Not in this millennium, we're told.

Billy Joel, joining dueling pianist Michael Cavanaugh at New York-New York's The Bar at Times Square in February 2001 for two songs: "With a Little Help From My Friends" and "Don't be Cruel." Joel obviously liked what he heard from Cavanaugh. When the Joel-inspired musical *Movin' Out* opened on Broadway, Cavanaugh took on Joel's role of singing narrator and was nominated for a Tony.

Rock singer **Pink** tattooing a penis onto the buttocks of Brannon Zimbleman, then creative director for AMP Salon, at Hart & Huntington Tattoo Company in Spring 2004.

Rap superstar **Eminem**, climbing onto the bar at Palms ghostbar and shouting, "Free drinks on the house!" while MTV cameras recorded it for a documentary in February 2004.

Julia Roberts and **Catherine Zeta-Jones** skinny-dipping at 5 a.m. with their body doubles in an outdoor Jacuzzi at the Hyatt Regency Lake Las Vegas after the "wrap" party for *America's Sweethearts* in February 2001.

Leonardo DiCaprio, **Adam Sandler** and **David Schwimmer** watching in amusement as **Adrian Young** of No Doubt stripped naked and jumped into the pool at the Rio's Maxim Lounge party in December 2001.

Elizabeth Taylor, wearing her 33-karat Krupp diamond ring and watching Siegfried & Roy's show on New Year's Eve 2001, with her dog Sugar, a Maltese, in the next seat.

A very, uh, "relaxed" **Paris Hilton**, heard singing "I Can't Get No Satisfaction" from the ladies stall at Palms ghostbar in September 2003. Upon exiting, at the request of a security guard, she noticed herself in the mirror, hiked up her dress, plopped down, cross-legged, and when told to leave, she suggested the security guard attempt the anatomically impossible.

 CELEBRITIES AT PLAY

Ben Affleck, flipping a $5,000 white chip to Mirage dealers and **Jennifer Lopez** retrieving it, putting it into her handbag and tossing out three $100 chips, during Thanksgiving weekend of 2002. Was it the beginning of the end?

Muhammad Ali demonstrating his "levitation" trick at the benefit screening of *Ali* at the Palms movie theaters in December 2001. "He won't say how he does it," said veteran fight promoter Bob Arum. "It's an optical illusion he's been performing for more than 30 years, and you'd swear he is off the ground."

Tom Cruise and **Nicole Kidman** whooping it up during repeated rides on the Stratosphere's Big Shot in late December 2000, a few weeks before their marriage went south.

Goateed actor **Johnny Depp** at Treasure Island's Mist lounge in a T-shirt, wool knit hat and glasses during a 2002 stopover. Depp, in Las Vegas after his plane got diverted, was filming *Pirates of the Caribbean* and decided to stay at the pirate-themed hotel. Now that's staying in character. No word on the grog he downed.

Leonardo DiCaprio spending half a day in the Palms video arcade, near the entrance to the hotel's movie multiplex, where his film *Catch Me If You Can* was playing in the winter of 2002. A lot of slack-jawed teenagers at the arcade went home with quite a tale.

Former Beatles **Paul McCartney** and **George Harrison**, and their significant others, chatting backstage with performers from Cirque du Soleil's *O* in February 2001.

Andre Agassi and **Steffi Graf** donning scuba gear and swimming with the dolphins at The Mirage's Dolphin Habitat before a crowd of surprised onlookers in September 1999, shortly after Graf moved in with Agassi.

Rene Charles, four months shy of his third birthday, trick or treating as Elvis with a microphone in hand with his parents **Celine Dion** and **Rene Angelil**, Halloween 2003.

Pamela Anderson in a black G-string and a white half-shirt, lounging outside her private cabana at the Hard Rock Hotel Beach Club pool in August 2000 with Swedish model **Marcus Schenkenberg**, who was celebrating his 32nd birthday. Floating near Anderson was a guy in a white Elvis jumpsuit, sideburns and gold-rimmed sunglasses. Need I say: definitely not together.

Most of the male cast members of the Sopranos being flashed by admiring female fans at the Golden Nugget pool in June 2004. Maybe they were auditioning to be Bada Bing girls.

 CELEBRITIES EAT TOO

Muhammad Ali, polishing off three bread pudding soufflés at N9NE inside the Palms while in town for the benefit screening of *Ali* in December 2001.

Tom Cruise and **Nicole Kidman**, sharing spicy Asian food and créme bruleé with carmelized bananas at Bellagio's Jasmine restaurant in late December 2000, shortly before Cruise filed divorce papers.

Vanna White, revealing to a certain eye-patched Las Vegas columnist how stuffed she was after dining at Bellagio's Picasso restaurant in January 2001. Lifting her shirt ever so carefully, she showed that the top button on her dress pants was unbuttoned and her zipper was down several inches.

Celine Dion, shopping for groceries at midnight with her husband **Rene Angelil** at the Wal-Mart Super Center in Henderson a few days before her March 2003 opening night at Caesars Palace.

Legendary chef **Julia Childs**, dining with a 40-member delegation from the Santa Barbara Museum of Art on a fine-dining tour in the spring of 2000. Starting at Bellagio, they made stops at Prime, Circo and Picasso, then moved to The Mirage to test the fare at Renoir.

Five-star chef **Julian Serrano** of Bellagio's Picasso, chowing down on fish tacos and churros at Rubio's Baja Grill on West Sahara Avenue with his wife Susan and daughter Estefania, shortly after being awarded his first five-star by *Mobil Guide* in January 2000.

Actress/model **Lauren Hutton**, receiving several herbal cocktails from her friends while being cared for at the University Medical Center. Hospital staffers had to confiscate the drinks because doctors were concerned the ingredients might neutralize her prescribed medicines. Hutton was hospitalized for almost three weeks in the fall of 2000 with serious injuries sustained after a motorcycle accident on State Route 167.

Proving you can take the boys out of the country, but you can't take grease out of their diet: star driver **Jeff Gordon**, strolling through the posh Bellagio the night before the 2003 NASCAR race in Las Vegas with a bag of McDonald's hamburgers and his gal pal.

Birthday boy **Leonardo DiCaprio**, being serenaded by his party of 20 at N9NE Steak House for his 28th birthday celebration during the Palms first anniversary weekend in November 2002. His pals, including **Tobey Maguire** and **Fred Durst** of Limp Bizkit, sang "For He's a Jolly Good Fellow" four times during the dinner.

Elaine Wynn, doing the drive-through at an In 'n Out Burger in her Bentley.

 ## CELEBRITIES IN LOVE

Los Angeles Lakers star **Kobe Bryant**, buying out three Bellagio restaurants on consecutive nights in April 2002 so he and his wife Vanessa could dine without distractions. A year later, Kobe's "distractions" cost him a lot more.

George Clooney and **Julia Roberts**, dancing hot-and-heavy at 3 a.m. in the Bellagio's Fontana Room during a champagne-fueled Oscar party for the three 2001 Academy Award winners involved in the *Ocean's Eleven* shoot, several days after the awards ceremony.

Demi Moore sitting on **Ashton Kutcher's** lap and "peppering him with kisses," according to a source, at Treasure Island's Kahunaville bar during a *Sirens of TI party* in July 2003.

A furious **Carmen Electra**, chucking ash trays at **Dennis Rodman** at the Crazy Horse Too strip club before they were married in November 1998. "And when they came in the next day, they were like newlyweds," says one of our spies.

Super-chef **Emeril Lagasse** and girlfriend **Alden Lovelace**, shopping for an engagement ring in late 1999 when — BAM! — there it was. Lagasse returned to Fred Leighton Rare Collectible Jewels in the Bellagio and purchased the four-carat rock set in an original 1930s art deco mounting.

Robert Goulet, serenading wife Vera on her birthday at the Bellagio's Fontana Lounge with "Some Enchanted Evening" and "This Nearly Was Mine." **Vince Falcone**, Frank Sinatra's longtime conductor, accompanied on the piano.

Tennis hottie **Anna Kournikova** and *Boogie Nights* star **Mark Wahlberg** spending some quality time in the *Real World* Suite at the Palms in February 2004. If she was trying to make boyfriend Enrique Iglasias jealous, it worked. A couple of weeks later, she was sporting a new mammoth pink diamond ring while recoupling with Iglasias in Australia. Game-set-match.

Vince Gill, wearing an Amy Grant T-shirt with her image on it during his show at Caesars Palace in November 1998, well before she announced her divorce from Christian singer Gary Chapman in June 1999. Gill and Grant married in March 2000.

Faith Hill and **Tim McGraw**, playing tonsil hockey on a darkened stage prior to a show at the MGM Grand in 1996, well before the public knew they were an item.

'N Sync's **Joey Fatone** getting the name of his fiancée Kelly tattooed on the inside of his lower lip (ouch!) at Hart & Huntington's Tattoo parlor in Spring 2004. The gesture came during Fatone's bachelor party weekend. Lance Bass attempted to get his own tattoo, but lasted only a couple of seconds before getting cold feet.

 ## GRATUITY HALL OF FAME

Ben Affleck twice gave away a reported $150,000 to dealers and cocktail servers at the Hard Rock Hotel, and bought a $150,000 Mercedes-Benz for J-Lo's mom.

Australian media mogul **Kerry Packer** sends ripples of electricity through town like no other whale because of his mega-tipping habits. "I've personally watched the man wager $200,000 a hand for the dealers," a dealer told me. "And they won, several times!" It is not an urban legend that Packer once gave a cocktail server a tip in excess of $100,000 and told her to "buy a new house."

Customers at a **Fatburger** franchise on the Strip were surprised to find a patron behind the counter, flipping hamburgers at 4 a.m. in October 2000. When the manager ordered the customer out of the kitchen, the man, a tipsy high roller fresh from a big score, reached inside his sports jacket, took out a bulging packet and doled out $100 bills to everyone in the fast-food restaurant. Three years later, a Major League Baseball owner approached me at Tabu and admitted he was the "player."

Monte Carlo magician **Lance Burton** didn't stop with treating 100 members of his cast and crew to a December 2000 holiday party at Planet Hollywood to celebrate their show's 2,000[th] performance. He also made $100 bills magically appear in the pockets of 10 Planet Hollywood servers.

Mike Tyson might be the Darth Vader of boxing to many fans, but some Las Vegas school kids know him for his soft-hearted side. After hearing that a group of underprivileged kids needed clothes for school, Tyson arranged to have a local store closed to the public so the kids could go on a shopping spree — on his tab.

George Clooney's generosity was evident during the *Ocean's Eleven* location shoots. While filming dinner scenes with **Julia Roberts** at Picasso in the Bellagio, Clooney overheard the crew talking about their dollar-a-day drawing. Seems the crew members write their names on dollar bills, toss them in a bowl and whomever's name is drawn at the end of the day wins the pot. Clooney tossed in $1,000. And Julia Roberts gave the winner a hug and kiss. Not a bad quinella.

Tennis lovebirds **Andre Agassi** and **Steffi Graf**, going unnoticed at Nobu's sushi bar in September 1999. Definitely noticed was another example of his legendary generosity. He tipped his server $25 on a $75 check and sent a C-note to the chef.

Hip-hop mogul **Sean "P. Diddy" Combs**, dropping three $100 bills as a tip in front of "Mr. Freeze," one of those human statues that wow tourists, at 2:40 a.m. outside Light, the Bellagio nightclub, in October 2003.

Dustin Hoffman, during the 1988 filming of *Rain Man* at Caesars Palace, was so pleased with the famed hamburgers (tenderloin trimmings mixed with ground chuck) at Caesars' Post-Time Deli that he went back for more; 240 more, for the film's cast and crew. The order was so large every restaurant in Caesars Palace was cooking burgers to go. The deli no longer exists.

Al Unser Jr., a two-time winner of the Indianapolis 500 and part-time Henderson resident, leaving $3,200 in chips in the tip jar for Kenny Saccomano and his musicians at the Round Bar at what was then the Resort at Summerlin in 2000.

 ## ATHLETES YOU'LL MOST LIKELY SEE

NBA great Charles Barkley — He is generous to a fault and so popular with the dealers that one of the blackjack tables in the MGM Grand's Mansion has an etched glass plaque that reads: "Reserved for Sir Charles."

Motocross Star Cary Hart – Las Vegas-born on-again, off-again boyfriend of rockstar Pink, is a fixture at Hart & Huntington's Tattoo Company which opened at the Palms Hotel in February 2004.

NHL star Jaromir Jagr — The Rio is a favorite spot for Jagr, who once had nearly $1 million riding on his bets.

Big-league brothers **Jason and Jeremy Giambi** — They live here and are off-season regulars at the Mandalay Bay's rumjungle nightclub.

Hall of Fame slugger Reggie Jackson — Jackson hasn't called Vegas home for long but already has a favorite nightspot: the ghostbar at the Palms.

NBA legend Michael Jordan — He loves to hang with Barkley and Tiger Woods at the MGM Grand tables and golf courses.

Duke basketball coach Mike Krzyzewski — Krzyzewski and his wife Mickie are regulars at Michael's, the gourmet restaurant at the Barbary Coast. One night after the restaurant closed, the Krzyzewskis watched as Peter Savarino proposed to their daughter Debbie at their table.

NBA star Shaquille O'Neal — Shaq is usually at the MGM Grand, but he was spotted one night in 2003 inside the deejay booth at Rain, the Palms' nightclub, throwing down sounds.

Boxer Mike Tyson — He's a regular at the Palms' ghostbar and The Venetian's V Bar. At the latter, he once took off his shoes and socks in the wee hours, and laid down in a booth for a nap. This was in the spring of 2003.

Golfer Tiger Woods — He's often seen at the MGM Grand's Mansion or the Rio's high-roller course, Secco Golf Club, where he used to tune up his game with then-coach Butch Harmon. Woods (surprise!) owns the course record at Rio Secco with a 64.

 CELEBRITY ALIASES

Singer **Marc Anthony** checked into a Las Vegas hotel in 2000 as "Justin Case."

Las Vegas headliner **Carrot Top** goes by "Bill Melater."

Johnny Depp, during the filming of *Fear and Loathing in Las Vegas*, went by "Johnny Stench."

Elton John's faves include "Sir Humphrey Handbag," "Lord Choc Ice," "Lord Elpus," "Binky Poodleclip," and "Sir Horace Pussy."

Michael Jordan has requested that he be addressed as "Mr. Sterling" while dining.

Jennifer Lopez was registered under "Jessica Rabbit" while staying with **Sean "Puff Daddy" Combs**, later **"P Diddy"** at the MGM Grand in 2000.

Lenny Kravitz requests "Zoe Isabella," his daughter's name.

Elvis Presley often went by "John Burrows."

Chicago Cubs slugger **Sammy Sosa** gave "Maximo Ali" as his fake name during Las Vegas visits.

Bruce Springsteen and wife **Patti Scialfa** went by "Bill and Patty Stevens" during his first Las Vegas concert in May 2000.

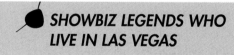

SHOWBIZ LEGENDS WHO LIVE IN LAS VEGAS

Marty Allen and **Steve Rossi**, of the Allen and Rossi comedy team.

Pat Cooper, stand-up comedian.

Buddy Greco, jazz-band leader.

Gladys Knight, rhythm and blues great.

BB King, blues icon.

Sonny King, lounge entertainer and Frank Sinatra pal.

Rich Little, impressionist.

Phyllis and **Christine McGuire**, from the singing McGuire Sisters

Pat Morita, actor (*The Karate Kid*) and comedian.

Mary Wilson, original member of The Supremes from 1958 to 1970.

 ## PLACES TO SPOT CELEBRITIES

Bellagio — The nightclub Light and the lounge Caramel draw the A-list crowd, as do the popular Picasso and Prime, and newly opened Fix restaurants.

Caesars Palace — Celine Dion's *A New Day* and Elton John's *The Red Piano*, located in the Colosseum, are celeb magnets. Bradley Ogden restaurant, across from the 4,000 seat venue, catches a ton of pre- and post-show action. Sighted: Michelle Pfeiffer, Barry Bonds, Michael Douglas and Catherine Zeta Jones, Tom Hanks, former President Bill Clinton, and Mike Piazza.

Hard Rock Hotel — Primo places to check out include a favorite among the Hollywood crowd, Nobu; Simon Kitchen & Bar; the high-roller salon, which has been frequented by Ben Affleck and Matt Damon; and Body English nightclub *Beacher's Madhouse Comedy Show* pulls in the bold-faced names, too.

Mandalay Bay — Baseball brothers Jason and Jeremy Giambi, who live in Las Vegas during the off-season, hang out at rumjungle a lot. Many entertainers head for the House of Blues Foundation Room and its private enclaves. Recently divorced Lisa Marie Presley and Nicolas Cage had tongues wagging when they hung out together in September 2003 after her first headliner here.

MGM Grand Hotel — Best bets, especially after a big on-property event, are Tabu and Studio 54. If Charles Barkley and Tiger Woods are prowling, Studio 54 is one of their main haunts. Barkley's been known to climb on the dance cube and shake his thang. Tom Jones dines at Nobhill.

The Forum Shops at Caesars — Whether fabulous shopping or fine dining, it is not unusual to find celebrities here. The Palm restaurant has long been a favorite watering hole and see-and-be-seen stop for the rich and famous. Sightings include Andre Agassi and wife Steffi Graf, and *Sopranos* castmates Steve Schirripa and John Ventimiglia. Wolfgang Puck's Spago is another prime territory. Big names include: Lance Armstrong, Robin Leach, Celine Dion, and NASCAR driver Jeff Gordon.

Palms — Aggressive marketing, launched by a party at the Playboy Club to reach out to the Hollywood crowd, made the Palms Celeb Central in 2002, it's first full year open. The ghostbar, Rain nightclub and N9NE steakhouse are happy hunting grounds. Leonardo DiCaprio celebrated his 28th birthday at N9NE, partied at Rain and stayed in the MTV *The*

Real World suite, as have Britney Spears and the high-profile sports duo of Serena Williams and Keyshawn Johnson.

Piero's Italian Cuisine — In another era, it was a mob scene, when it was known as Villa D'Este. New owner Freddie Glusman changed the name, but not the vibe. Sightings include Jerry Lewis (usually in tennis shorts, white socks and carrying a bottle of wine), George Clooney, Mike Tyson, Stevie Van Zandt, and Jerry Tarkanian.

New York New York — *Newsweek* dubbed Cirque du Soleil's *Zumanity* as Cirque du Risque. From first blush, it is the sexiest production to hit Sin City. This den of seduction lures many a celebrity, and some of their girlfriends have ended up on stage in the orgy scene. Since its opening in 2003, celebrity guests have included Paris and Nicky Hilton, Hugh Hefner and his bevy of blondes, Ashton Kutcher and Demi Moore.

Venetian — Numerous NFL- and NBA-associated conventions are held here, making it a target-rich environment. Mike Tyson is V bar habitué.

 LOCAL CLAIMS TO FAME

The comedic duo of **Allen & Rossi** (Marty Allen and Steve Rossi) appeared on the *Ed Sullivan Show* 44 times, including three times with The Beatles.

Harrah's headliner **Clint Holmes** had a Top 40 hit, "Playground in My Mind," that spent two weeks at No. 2 in 1973. It stayed in the Top 40 for 15 weeks.

David Copperfield claims he has 80,000 magic items stored in "a top secret location in Nevada." His most prized possession is the only recording of Harry Houdini's voice, made almost 75 years ago. Copperfield told New York gossip reporter Baird Jones he paid millions for the recording. "I was shocked because Houdini's voice is very high-pitched and shrill, without the powerful presence I had expected." Houdini died the day his voice was recorded by his friend Thomas Edison.

Las Vegas Mayor **Oscar Goodman** regularly attended Dick Clark's *American Bandstand* while growing up in Philadelphia. "Yeah, I danced on the show but mostly we went down there to fight."

Steve Lawrence and **Eydie Gorme** showbiz icons toured with Frank Sinatra for an entire year, 1990-1991.

Greg Maddux, Las Vegas Valley High School graduate of 1984, went on to win an unprecedented four Cy Young Awards in consecutive seasons with the Chicago Cubs and Atlanta Braves (1992-1995).

Broadway and opera star **Paige O'Hara** gave her voice to Belle, Disney's animated heroine in the Oscar-winning film *Beauty and the Beast*.

Former Jubilation bouncer **Steve Schirripa** parlayed his connections as entertainment director at the Riviera into a regular role on *The Sopranos* as Bobby "Bacala" Baccalieri, Uncle Junior's right-hand man.

Longtime Elvis impersonator **Pete Willcox** has fooled even the King: "When Fonz hits the jukebox in *Happy Days* and Elvis' (song) 'Hounddog' starts playing, that's my voice. Elvis told me he thought it was his voice."

Headline this: "You talkin' to me?" Former Las Vegas One reporter **Ann Yeager** had just covered **Robert DeNiro's** bid for a liquor license at his new restaurant Nobu (Hard Rock Hotel) in 1999 when she got the call of her career. DeNiro's publicist reached her in the newsroom and informed Yeager that DeNiro requested her presence for dinner. She joined him and his group at Nobu, and was later seen leaving the restaurant with him.

 ## CELEBRITY STIFFS (Worst Tippers)

Bill Gates — Mr. Microtips.

Michael Jordan — Dealers have code named him "Hoardin' Jordan."

Phil Mickelson — After winning $560,000 on a futures bet (he took the Baltimore Ravens at 28-1 odds to win the 2001 Super Bowl), he walked out of the Bellagio sports book without leaving a dime. But I'm told he has a solid record as a tipper.

Scotty Pippen — His detractors refer to him as "No Tippin' Pippen."

Pete Rose — The Hit King walks a lot.

Britney Spears — The classic: After a comped lunch for three, that included her server at Gordon Biersch Brewing Company dashing off to a Starbucks to get her favorite coffee drink, Britney kept her virginity as a non-tipper. She not only didn't toke for the lunch, but she stiffed the server for the cost of the coffee.

Will Smith — Known locally as "Will Stiff."

Jerry Tarkanian — Master of the Vegas fast-break.

Bruce Willis — A diehard gambler; a dud of a tipper.

Tiger Woods — His fan club doesn't include many dealers. He took Mandalay Bay for $250,000-plus one night in 2001, then took a hike. At the MGM Grand Mansion, while playing for $10,000 a hand, he gave a cocktail server $5. But when his girlfriend mentioned the server had been tipped, he pulled back the fiver.

SPORTS CELEBRITIES WITH HOMES IN VEGAS

Bob Arum, legendary boxing promoter.

Randall Cunningham, NFL quarterback.

Jason Giambi, New York Yankees.

Greg Maddux, four-time Cy Young Award-winning pitcher.

Napoleon McCallum, former Navy and NFL running back.

Jonathan Ogden, Baltimore Ravens All-Pro offensive lineman.

Al Unser Jr., Indy car driver.

Jerry Tarkanian, UNLV college basketball coach.

Mike Tyson, heavyweight boxer.

Dick Williams, three-time World Series manager.

 ## LAS VEGAS' FAVORITE CHARACTERS

Mayor Oscar Goodman — For years he charmed juries as one of the top mob attorneys. In 1999 he turned to politics and won going away. Everybody loves Raymond . . . and Oscar.

Dr. Lonnie Hammargren — What other city's former lieutenant governor is a neurosurgeon, collector of Old Vegas memorabilia to the extreme (his home has been featured in articles and television) and honorary consul-general of Belize.

Fred Glusman —This rough-edged owner of Piero's Italian Ristorante banned boxing promoter Bob Arum from his restaurant for two years over a spat involving boxing tickets (Glusman thought he deserved better seats; Arum suspected Glusman was scalping them). Glusman rubbed salt in the wound by having a painting done showing himself with Don King, Arum's ultimate rival. But it was all in fun. Well, some of it. All in all, his bark is worse than his bite.

Sonny King — Nobody's hung out with more Old Vegas royalty than King, storyteller extraordinaire. He roomed with Dean Martin, worked with Jimmy Durante for 28 years and was one of Sinatra's goombahs. Sinatra was more than a friend of 50 years; he was godfather of King's daughter Antoinette.

Robin Leach — This former host of the *Lifestyles of the Rich and Famous* television show is still a globe-trotting bon vivant and has kept champagne sales popping since buying a home here in 1999. When he's not doing his day job as a consultant, he's living the life as Vegas' ultimate Man About Town. The party isn't "official" until Robin walks in with his top-heavy posse.

Cook E. Jarr — This lounge legend is one of those characters who's never out of character and, best of all, he lives up to all the glitz and connects with crowds. A 2003 inductee into the Casino Hall of Fame, he performs weekends at Harrah's Carnaval Court.

Phyllis McGuire — A member of the legendary McGuire Sisters, Phyllis liked her men a little rough around the edges. Her longtime relationship with mobster Sam Giancana was turned into the 1995 TV movie, *Sugartime.* In the 1990s she ran with gaming maverick Bob Stupak, who sent her 1,001 roses. Elvis made his interest known, too, but the feeling wasn't mutual. "He was pursuing me. I wasn't interested, I truly wasn't," McGuire told me on the 25th anniversary of Elvis' death. "I was with Sam then. I used to tell anybody that came up to me, 'Don't bother; you'll end up in the bottom of Lake Mead.' "The former preacher's daughter spent a night in the cooler in 1999 after Las Vegas police claim she head-butted and kicked an officer who pulled over her Cadillac.

Monti Rock III — You can't miss this gadfly around the local scene, dressed in his leopard-print and driving a Ford Focus with these words printed on the back and side: "In this car drives a legend in his own mind." A celebrity hairdresser-turned-disco-diva, he sold seven million copies of the disco record "Get Dancin' " as Disco Tex and the Sex-o-Lettes. A shameless self-promoter, he played himself as a deejay in *Saturday Night Fever* and was on *The Tonight Show* 84 times over 17 years. He wears what appears to be a stuffed cat draped over one shoulder. Why? We're afraid to ask.

Bob Stupak — High-stakes gambler, dreamer and schemer, Stupak built Vegas World casino from scratch then took his ambitions to loftier heights by constructing the Stratosphere Tower. When he isn't scrapping with the gaming control board, suing over moon rocks, he's up to another political shenanigan. Suspicious minds think he was pulling the strings that got his nurse-turned-girlfriend Janet Moncrief elected to city council in 2003.

Jerry Tarkanian — Tark the Shark will always have a special place in the hearts of Las Vegas fans for the lofty heights he took UNLV's basketball program. When Vegas lost Elvis' electricity, Tark and his teams filled the void in the 1970s, 1980s and early 1990s.

 ## MOST FAMOUS RESIDENTS

Andre Agassi and **Steffi Graf**, tennis stars.

Susan Anton, actress and singer.

Tony Curtis, film star.

Celine Dion, singer.

Robert Goulet, singer and Broadway star.

BB King, blues guitarist.

Jerry Lewis, film icon.

Siegfried & Roy, magicians.

Steve Lawrence and **Eydie Gorme**, singers.

Greg Maddux, baseball pitcher.

 ## THE RICH ARE DIFFERENT

Barbra Streisand had the MGM Grand remodel her high-roller suite with furniture and art shipped in from her California home for the week of her New Year's Eve 1999 performances. In addition, she requested that no hotel employees have eye contact with her.

Andre Agassi and **Steffi Graf** once placed a to-go order for raw steak from the Bellagio's Prime restaurant and took it home for a cookout shortly after she joined him here in September 1999.

Julia Roberts tossed a wrap party in the summer of 2000 for *The Mexican* film cast at Mandalay Bay's wave pool and asked that the waves be twice the size of the previous wrap party held by co-star **Brad Pitt**.

George Clooney's high-roller suite at the Bellagio was equipped with a Guinness beer dispensing system during the 2001 filming of *Ocean's Eleven*. Clooney, Brad Pitt and Ben Affleck had the beer systems in their California homes.

Celine Dion and **Rene Angelil** get first prize for the most over-the-top Vegas wedding, and it wasn't even their first trip down the aisle but a renewal of vows. The January 2000 ceremony took place in a Caesars Palace ballroom that had been transformed into an ancient mosque. The party for 200-plus guests included six Berber tents set among live desert animals. The five-course feast was prepared by chefs from Montreal, Lebanon and Syria. Price tag: $1.5 million.

Caesars Palace was chocoholic heaven at one high-roller party in early 2001. A toga party included a processional of centurions carting in a nearly nude chocolate-covered Goddess of Chocolate.

When **Nicolas Cage** was filming *Con Air* here in 1996, his contract stipulated that he would get to sleep in his own bed each night. So, during one lengthy stretch of night shoots, he was flown to Burbank about dawn every morning on a private jet.

Jet-setting actor **George Hamilton**, the man with the year-round tan, loves the sun so much that he reportedly had a sunshine clause in his contract at a Las Vegas resort in the 1980s. It stipulated that if the weather was cloudy or bad on his day off, his employer would fly him to a city with a sunny forecast.

A high roller at the Imperial Palace tipped valet Walt Trantini $100 for bringing up his Mercedes. Good thing Trantini didn't spend it. The big spender returned 90 minutes later and asked if he could have the $100 back. "He said he got to Whiskey Pete's (in Primm, Nevada), stopped for something to eat and realized he only had a dollar — and no credit cards," said Trantini, who coughed up the C-note and got a $10 tip in return.

Robin Leach, long time host of the *Lifestyles of the Rich & Famous*, and one of his blondes du jour at Planet Hollywood (Forum Shops at Caesars) sharing a bottle of Dom Perignon and Captain Crunch chicken wings. "Champagne wishes and chicken wing dreams" doesn't quite have the proper ring.

WHAT THE STARS DRINK IN SIN CITY

Former Motley Crue bad boy **Tommy Lee** downed three Patron Silver tequila shots with wine during dinner at Fix (Bellagio) the night he got bounced out of Light in June 2004 during a deejay gig that went sour.

LeBron James — Toasting his NBA Rookie of the Year selection at the Palms' N9NE Steak house with an age-appropriate cocktail of ginger ale mixed with Coca Cola.

When megarappers **Eminem** and **50 Cent** had dinner at N9NE Steak House (Palms) in early 2004, guess who ordered the strawberry daiquiri and who knocked down Patron? Somebody's got to tell 50 Cent daiquiris are froo-froo drinks, but it won't be me.

George Clooney — Ketel One vodka with cranberry, and Skyy vodka and tonic at Whiskey Bar, Green Valley Ranch.

Mike Tyson — Has gone down for the count with Dom Perignon at V Bar (Venetian).

Lance Bass — The 'N Sync singer has asked for "Sex with an Alligator" shots at Light. To get crocked, apparently.

Leonardo DiCaprio — Grey Goose vodka and tonic at the Palms Hotel.

Lennox Lewis — Cosmopolitan, with this twist: The heavyweight champ told a host at Light, the Bellagio nightclub, that he has a thing about clinking glasses during a toast because someone could put something in his drink, pointing out it was done during medieval times as "a method to poison your brethren when the glasses touched."

Kid Rock — Coors Light and Jack Daniels at Tabu (MGM Grand).

Britney Spears — Purple Hooter shots at House of Blues Foundation Room (Mandalay Bay) with brothers George and Phil Maloof.

CELEBRITY WEDDINGS

George Clooney and **Talia Balsam** — December 15, 1989, at the White Lace and Promises Chapel.

Kirk Douglas and **Parisian Ann Buydens** — May 28, 1954, at the Sahara.

Clint Eastwood and TV news anchor **Dina Ruiz** — March 31, 1996, at Shadow Creek, the ultra-exclusive, once-private golf club built by casino developer Steve Wynn.

Richard Gere and supermodel **Cindy Crawford** — December 12, 1991, at the Little Church of the West Chapel.

Britney Spears and **Jason Alexander** – January 3, 2004, at the Little White Wedding Chapel.

Michael Jordan and **Juanita Vanoy** — September 2, 1989, at The Little White Chapel.

Paul Newman and **Joanne Woodward** — January 29, 1958, at the El Rancho.

Elvis Presley and **Priscilla Beaulieu** — May 1, 1967, at the Aladdin.

Mickey Rooney and **Ava Gardner** — January 10, 1942, at the Little Church of the West.

Frank Sinatra and **Mia Farrow** — July 19, 1966, at the Sands.

 ## TOP WEDDING CHAPELS FOR THE FAMOUS (and less-famous)

Caesars Palace — The Terrazza Garden is an intimate palm-surrounded setting for parties of fewer than 50. The surroundings include a Romanesque temple, a koi pond/fountain and a unique stone-tiled aisle. Mark Grace of the Arizona Diamondbacks got hitched here in January 2002; Kenyon Martin of the New Jersey Nets did likewise in 2003. **702-731-7422**

Candlelight Wedding Chapel — The second-busiest chapel in town is across from Circus-Circus. Celebrities married here include Ray Liotta, Whoopi Goldberg, Bette Midler, Bob Seger and *The Lone Ranger* himself, Clayton Moore. 2855 Las Vegas Blvd. South. **702-735-4179**

Chapel by the Bay — Ricky Martin walked his future sister-in-law down the aisle at his brother's 1999 wedding. John Taylor of Duran Duran took the trip to the altar here in 1999. Charisma Carpenter of *Buffy the Vampire Slayer* found hallowed ground amid the vaulted ceilings and French windows. There's a courtyard of palm trees and a fountain for the wedding shots. Mandalay Bay. **702-632-7490**

The Wedding Chapel at Bellagio — If getting married in a mini-palace is your dream, this chapel heavy on ornate European décor is it. Bellagio. **702-693-7111**.

Little Chapel of the Flowers — Hosting 7,000-to-8,000 weddings a year undoubtedly influenced a No. 1 ranking by *Bride's* magazine. "We're not the 'slam-bam, thank you Ma'am' chapel,' " says publicist Miriam Reed. "We're extremely traditional." Even those well-known traditionalists Dennis Rodman and Carmen Electra married here. 1717 Las Vegas Blvd. South. **702-735-4331**.

Flamingo Garden Chapel — This stunning tropical setting is one of the most romantic sites in Las Vegas. There are waterfalls, flamingos, lagoons, rosebushes and birds (of paradise, natch). Flamingo. **702-733-3232**.

Graceland Wedding Chapel — Jon Bon Jovi tied the knot here even if Elvis didn't (that happened at the old Aladdin). In fact, Graceland is strictly BYOE — bring your own Elvis — since the chapel's only association with The King is the name of his Memphis compound. It was, however, the first to exploit the association and introduce Elvis weddings. 619 Las Vegas Blvd. South. **702-824-5732**.

Little Church of the West — It claims to be the oldest building on the Strip; when the old Hacienda closed, the church was loaded up and moved to where it now sits across from Mandalay Bay. This 60-year-old business also claims to have recorded five times as many celebrity weddings as any place in the world. Among them: Billy Bob Thornton and Angelina Jolie; Judy Garland; Dudley Moore; and David Cassidy. 4617 Las Vegas Blvd. South. **1-800-821-2452** or **702-739-7971**.

Princess Wedding Chapel — Themed princess weddings reign here, including Princess Diana and Elvis in the Castle (no, not together). The stunning gazebos surely helped it get named for best weddings by the *Review-Journal*. Greek Isles Hotel and Casino; **1-800-823-3435** or **702-967-0045**.

Little White Wedding Chapel — It has been the runaway leader in weddings for years (averaging 500 per day). And that was before all of the publicity from Britney Spears' quickie with Jason Alexander on January 3, 2004. The Little White Wedding Chapel is open 24/7, and many celebrities show up unannounced, like the party of six that arrived by cab at 2:30 a.m. on September 2, 1989. It was some guy named Michael Jordan and bride-to-be Juanita Vanoy. It even has a drive-thru for those who want to be hitched in a hurry. 1301 Las Vegas Blvd. South. **702-382-3546**.

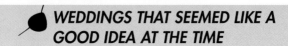

Christina Applegate, who played Kelly Bundy on *Married . . . With Children*, announced in 1996 that she ran off to Las Vegas and married another woman. "We took it very seriously; rings, rice, the whole bit." But, she's quick to add, no sex was involved. "We did it to prove that the bond between two women surpasses the bond between two men." Applegate later married Johnathon Schaech, from the film *That Thing You Do*, in 2001.

Broadway icon **Carol Channing** married Las Vegas advertising and television executive Charles Lowe at a Boulder City, Nevada, ceremony in July 1956. In divorce papers, Channing claimed she and Lowe only had sex "once or twice in our 41-year marriage and that was 41 years ago." She claimed she stuck to her wedding vows during the entire marriage.

Basketball bizarro **Dennis Rodman** and MTV hottie **Carmen Electra**, after briefly dating, made a fastbreak for The Chapel of the Flowers on November 15, 1998. Rodman's attorney called a timeout, claiming his client was too drunk to know what he was doing. They split after nine days. She divorced him in April 1999.

Oscar winners **Angelina Jolie** and **Billy Bob Thornton** wed on May 5, 2000. A short time later she was sporting a tattoo of a dragon with the words "Billy Bob" above it. After she filed for divorce from Thornton on July 18, 2002, the tattoo was reworked to obliterate Billy Bob's name.

Guns 'N Roses frontman **Axl Rose** (real name William Bailey) married Erin Everly in Las Vegas in April 1990. They divorced later that year.

Britney's 55-hour mistake. A trip through the buffet lasted longer than this honeymoon.

Charo (real name Maria Rosario Pilar Martinez Molina, now Rasten) married bandleader **Xavier Cugat**, the "King of Rumba," on August 7, 1966. They were the first couple married at Caesars Palace. Depending on which birth certificate you believe — she once filed federal documents amending her birth date — Charo was either 15 or 25; he was 66.

Mickey Rooney, 21, married **Ava Gardner**, 19, in January 1942. They lasted a year and a week. Rooney, the king of Vegas weddings, also tied the knot here with the following: Betty Jane Rase in 1944, Martha Vickers in 1948, Elaine Mahnken in 1952, Barbara Ann Thompson in 1958, Marge Lane in 1967, Carolyn Hockett in 1969 and January Chamberlin in 1978.

Darva Conger and **Rick Rockwell** tied the knot on the FOX TV special *Who Wants to Marry a Millionaire?* in 2000 at the Las Vegas Hilton. She received an annulment in Clark County a couple of months later, saying she "wanted her dignity back."

Magicians **Lance Burton** and **Melinda**, "The First Lady of Magic," were married briefly in 1993 before the magic faded.

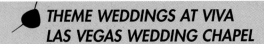

— **"Me Tarzan, you Jane."** Or if that doesn't excite, there's always **"Me Spock, you Uhuru."** It doesn't matter what your fantasy, the Viva Las Vegas Wedding Chapel has a themed wedding to fulfill it. Figure that so many chapel weddings are second marriages, a lot of brides and grooms already have been there, done that when it comes to tuxedos and white lace. It's doubtful, however, the same packages could be said of the following themes:

— In the **Beach Party**, the bikini-clad (optional) bride gets carried down the aisle on a surfboard by two muscle men. A Big Kahuna dude officiates.

— **Elvis' Blue Hawaii** is the chapel's most popular themed wedding. It includes Elvis memorabilia; Hawaiian sets and props; an Elvis impersonator as minister; hula dancers, showgirls or a Priscilla impersonator. Elvis sings "Hawaiian Wedding Song" and girls do hula.

— In the **Gangster** wedding a "Godfather" minister accompanied by two bodyguards officiates. A singing waiter bustles around a table decorated with chianti and grapes. The "Godfather" sets the mood with "Ole Solo Mio." Cold feet? Fuhgetaboutit.

— The **Intergalactic** beams Mr. Spock into the ceremony through a magical illusion. Couples usually rent Starfleet outfits. Special effects include theatrical lighting and laser beams.

— "When people ask for a **tacky wedding** this is usually what we give them and it's a big seller," owner/operator Ron De Car says of the Las Vegas Game Show theme. Elvis usually performs the ceremony, which includes a cocktail waitress serving drinks and a dealer who rolls the dice to decide who says the vows first.

 VEGAS FACTOID

Retired actor **Dick Wilson**, of the Las Vegas suburb Henderson, was on a roll longer than the hottest Vegas dice player. Wilson spent 25 years as Mr. Whipple, the bifocals-wearing, bow-tied TV pitchman who exhorted, "Please do not squeeze the Charmin." But Mr. Whipple apparently put the squeeze on Procter & Gamble, the Cincinnati-based maker of Charmin, when his lifetime supply of the bathroom tissue stopped arriving in 1995. "All of a sudden it just stopped, and I don't know why," Wilson told The Associated Press in 1995. "I thought maybe I should write them a Happy Christmas card, because maybe they thought I was dead." In no time, Mr. Whipple was well-stocked in Charmin after Procter & Gamble took care of the oversight. Wilson turned 88 in 2004.

 VEGAS FACTOID

Most nights Cappozoli's restaurant serves up everything Italian. Some nights, they serve up nonstop slices of Old Vegas. The legendary **Tom Jones** walked in at 2:30 a.m.

one morning with local lounge hero **Cook E. Jarr**. Three hours later, Jones was still on stage, a champagne glass in one hand and a microphone in the other, belting out Elvis and Sinatra hits, along with his own chart-busters such as "Delilah." Joining Jones on stage were Jarr, Harrah's headliner **Clint Holmes**, Stardust musical impressionist **Bob Anderson**, comedian **Dennis Blair** and Elvis impersonator **Pete Wilcox**."This was a throwback to the Old Vegas days," said Holmes. "You couldn't walk through the bar. "I left at 5:25 and Tom was still on stage," he added.

 VEGAS FACTOID

A Las Vegas limo driver got some advice from New York Yankees manager **Joe Torre** on how to play the field. The twenty-something chauffeur had spent much of the day shuttling Torre around town to a number of events in early 2000. Torre overheard several telephone calls between the driver and a friend that involved the driver's sad story of love gone bad. When the day ended, Torre climbed out of the car, shook hands with the driver and put both hands on the young man's shoulders. "In matters of the heart," said Torre, "the hardest decision can be whether to stay with the starter or go to the pen. "If it's not this one, the next one will be the closer."

Howard Hughes, a compulsive hygiene freak, washing his shirt in a water fountain on the Stardust golf course.

 VEGAS FACTOID

Okay, they're not celebrities, but they're in my "It's Vegas Baby" Hall of Fame: Cabbie Gerry Mazur was driving down the Strip in April 2001, when two vans stopped in front of him near Caesars Palace. Faster than you can say "naked as a jaybird," the van doors flew open and a dozen occupants wearing only their birthday suits dashed to Caesars' famed fountains for a quick dip, than raced back to their vehicles for a quick getaway. "I thought I've seen strange things out here — and strange things that happened in the cab — but nothing like this," said Mazur.

Chapter 3

Sin City

Las Vegas hasn't strayed far from its Sin City roots since gambling was legalized in 1931. Oh sure, the mob scene that Benjamin "Bugsy" Siegel first brought to the desert in the 1940s was all but gone, or underground, by the 1980s. There was a brief flirtation with kids' stuff in the 1990s, but then it was back to the basics. Skin has never been more in.

Gordon Biersch Brewing Company — Fridays are huge. You'll find a friendly, flirty crowd from the 20-somethings to middle-aged suits. "Definitely a local meat market; you feel like you're on a runaway," said one of my female spies. 3987 Paradise Road. **702-312-5247**

Drai's Afterhours — One of Sin City's most popular destinations. On the nights (mornings) I've been there, this monument to after-hours debauchery has it all: from celebs to strippers, showgirls to sophisticates, all partying to a primal beat in this stylish nightclub inside the Barbary Coast. The action starts at midnight, Wednesdays through Sundays only. Barbary Coast. **702-737-0555**

ghostbar — Hip and sensuous, the Palms' ghostbar has a high-energy vibe and a bevy of gorgeous cocktail servers in all-white uniforms with very short shorts. A-plus atmosphere and an awe-inspiring panorama of the Strip. "The last time I was there, somebody invited me to Europe," said a local hottie. Plan B: Tuesday's pool parties down on the ground at the Palms' Skin pool lounge attract the thong crowd. The Palms. **702-942-7777**

Hard Rock Hotel — Rock and roll! The party usually starts at the pool, moves to the legendary center bar and really heats up at Body English, where actions speak louder than words. In case your panties go missing, there's a Love Jones lingerie shop. Rehab Sundays at the pool, with hip hop and a sea of hotties, ain't no Betty Ford Clinic. **702-693-5000**

House of Blues Foundation Room — This private club on the penthouse level of Mandalay Bay attracts the upscale and more than a few California poseurs. Getting lucky here is undoubtedly a lot easier than getting a drink at the notoriously understaffed bar. Mandalay Bay. **702-632-7631**

Light — This well-appointed Bellagio hotspot attracts the look-at-me-crowd and there's a lot to see. Lasting image: Paris Hilton getting a piggyback ride from Brian Urlacher, All-Pro middle linebacker for the Chicago Bears, in September 2003. Light's management put up a billboard on Flamingo Road in the fall of 2003 showing four poodles on a poolside chaise lounge. It sported the wording, "The bitches and I will be there." It lasted three days. Bellagio. **702-693-8300**

Rain — It's raining men and chicks at this water-walled, over-the-top dance club inside the Palms. The biggest crowds in town make it a happy hunting ground. Get in line early or it will be a long wait. The Palms. **702-942-7777**

rumjungle — Everything's big about this place: the crowds, the rum drinks, and especially the sound, thanks to the 18-foot conga drums. The price of closing the deal at this singles spot could be temporary deafness. Mandalay Bay. **702-632-7408**

Studio 54 — For the most part it's a 20-something hip-hop crowd, but those who lived through the disco era will feel right at home from 10 p.m. to midnight, when the music covers the '70s, '80s and '90s. After that, this MGM Grand hotspot is "a teeming mass of body bonding," according to a habitué of hot clubs. MGM Grand Hotel. **702-891-7254**

Whiskey Bar and Whiskey Beach — Formerly Whiskey Sky, this indoor/outdoor nightclub in suburban Henderson is a popular alternative for those who want nothing to do with traffic clogging the Strip. Well-known nightclub operator Rande Gerber made sure it's a sexy playground: a giant video screen features women kissing. Green Valley Ranch, 2300 Paseo Verde Parkway, Henderson. **702-617-7777**

 ## HOTTEST COCKTAIL UNIFORMS

BiKiNiS — At Bikinis, inside the Rio, the tops are barely bigger than an eyepatch.

Hard Rock Hotel — The black lingerie look at Body English is better than the little blue pill. the leopard skin vests, sheer tops and leather shorts in the casino still make men purr.

Imperial Palace — If Hugh Hefner follows through on his plans to open a Playboy Club with a retro bunny look in Las Vegas, the IP might be hearing from Hef's attorneys. The Imperial Palace has copied the bunny uniforms for years.

Mandalay Bay — The front takes a plunge of NASDAQ proportions and the backside is classic wedgy wear.

New York-New York — Hubba-Hubba.

Rio — When the Rio opened in January 1990, it set the bar for the sexiest look, ranking No. 1 for years. Comedian David Gee said it best after an October 1999 earthquake jolted Las Vegas: "It was such a temblor that cocktail waitresses at the Rio fell back into their uniforms." A tamer new look came along in May 2003 when management introduced the "BevErtainer" — part server, part entertainer — but it's still a Top 10 entry.

Palms Skin Pool Lounge — It's called Skin for a reason.

Studio 54 — What goes with a flashing disco ball? The million-dollar bra done with fake diamonds, Christina Aguilera's style of miniskirts, go-go boots and nude fishnet stockings, of course.

Tabu — The winner: the sheer lace mini-dress over thong undies. They fit perfectly in the outrageously opulent and sensual surroundings of this elite lounge inside the MGM

The Venetian — Not the Venice I remember. The Italian-inspired casino took the Rio's early blueprint and fleshed it out.

Most strip clubs have a $10-$20 cover charge, although you'd think a guy with an eye patch would get in for half price.

Cheetah's Topless Club — Wanna meet Mike Tyson but not in the ring? For years this has been the former heavyweight boxing champion's home-away-from-home and one of the few girlie clubs where he hasn't worn out his welcome. He spent so much time here he was best man at the wedding of one of its hosts. Consider this a forewarning: He's not Mr. Hospitable. "He'll pay people to go away," a spy told me. "He gave a customer $200 to go away." One day he showed up and invited the girls outside to see his new Lamborghini. "He's always asking the girls for their phone numbers." 2112 Western Ave.. **702-384-0074**.

Crazy Horse Too — Name a sports celeb and they've been here, hanging with owner Rick Rizzolo. Hollywood also has a fondness for the place: *Ocean's Eleven* scenes with Brad Pitt were filmed here in the spring of 2001, and George Clooney was seen leaving in a limo at 6 a.m. in April, 2003. 2476 Industrial Road. **702-382-8003**.

Club Paradise — Location, location, location. No topless club in town has it better than Club Paradise, directly across Paradise Road from the Hard Rock Hotel. The steady stream of celebrities include Howard Stern and his cast of characters, who camp out here during their annual road trips to broadcast from the Hard

Rock. George Clooney, I'm told, is a $20-a-drink tipper. A member of a venerable rock group tipped two girls $2,000 and asked them to join him later in his suite at the Hard Rock. When they didn't show, he called Club Paradise management and demanded his money back. A member of the U.S. Olympic hockey team flew in from the Salt Lake City Winter Games on a day off to unwind. 4416 Paradise Road. **702-734-7990**.

Deja Vu Showgirls — Peeler/groupie Alison Rowse — stage name: Sianna — put this all-nude, no-alcohol club on the world map when she spent the night with The Who's John Entwistle, who was found dead in his Hard Rock Hotel room in June 2002 from cocaine-induced heart problems. 3247 Industrial Road. **702-894-4167**.

Jaguars — You can't miss it if you take Desert Inn Road. There are so many bright lights it sticks out like a working girl in church. But there's nothing cheap about the money that went into what the owners consider the Taj Mahal of strip clubs. The federal G-Sting operation shut it down for a while in 2004. My favorite Jaguar story: His aging Jaguar needed some repairs, so Terry Head, long-time local entertainer, started searching his telephone directory. After four attempts, he was ready to call it quits when he decided to make one more call. A honey-voiced young lady was confused when Head asked, "Do you service old Jaguars?" 3355 Procyon St.. **702-732-1116**.

Olympic Garden — On weekends, it's one of the world's busiest clubs, with 200 ladies working the room. There's also a male revue upstairs for the ladies. OG's halftime show during Monday Night Football is a sight to behold. The Dennis Rodman freak show stopped here on a regular basis. 1531 Las Vegas Blvd. South. **702-385-8987**.

Sapphire — Robin Leach said it best when he called this 71,000-square-foot monstrosity "the 52 double-D of men's clubs." Then, after sizing it up on opening night in early 2003, he had to leave before tops started popping so he didn't violate various morals clauses in his TV contracts. "We were told it would be 600 girls and 6,000 guys," said dancer Angela of Cleveland, who was in for the weekend. "I've been doing this for 19 years, and I've never seen a club like this. Nobody's going to touch it for a long, long time." About 300 girls are working during the busiest weekends. 3025 S. Industrial Road. **702-796-6000**.

Spearmint Rhino — A certain Hollywood hunk spent a lot of time here getting over an overly publicized romance. He dropped a bundle on his favorite ballerina while hiding out in one of the three celebrity VIP rooms, complete with their own dance floors. 3340 S. Highland Ave. **702-796-3600**.

Striptease Upscale Gentlemen's Club — This is one of the classier clubs, thanks to a major expansion that almost quadrupled its space in 2002. If the bouncer looks familiar, he's probably one of those beefy twins who tailed George Clooney in *Ocean's Eleven*. Amenities include a "shower stage" and two VIP rooms. 3750 Valley View Blvd.. **702-253-1555**.

Treasures — When it opened in September 2003, Treasures was billed as the Bellagio of local gentlemen's clubs. Management claims the $30-million investment makes it the most expensive club in the world. Motorists on Interstate 15 can glimpse a few of the 100 custom-made Greek statues and bronze artworks. As many as 300 dancers are projected for busy nights. The opening-night crowd reminded me of an old Vegas line: "If you're indicted, you're invited." A month after it opened, former NBA badboy Dennis Rodman slam-dunked a motorcycle into a parking lot pole. 2801 Westwood Drive. **702-257-3030**.

 ## SEXIEST SHOWS & PARTIES

Chippendales: The Show — The things I've heard women scream at this show! It became Bachelorette Central almost instantly. Twelve near-perfect male specimens strut their sensual stuff without crossing the line. Las Vegas twins Ethel Ciulla and Helen Del Hoyo showed up for their 80th birthday in March 2003 and promised to be back for their 85th. They were offered free tickets for life from Chippendales. Rio, 3700 W. Flamingo Road. **702-252-7776**.

Las Vegas Fetish and Fantasy Halloween Ball — More than 4,000 adults celebrated their fantasies at All American Sports Park in 2002. Everyone from adult film stars to snake charmers and fire breathers took the stage before a raucous, fun crowd. No wonder it was voted "One of the Top 10 Parties in the World" by the Travel Channel.

Fetish & Fantasy St. Valentine's Ball — Cupid and the Devil party hearty 9 p.m. till dawn. Locations vary; check **702-942-7777** or **www.cluberotica.net**.

La Femme — Pronounced "La Fahm," this import from Paris was part of the first wave of change at the start of the 21st century, when Vegas decided to return to its sexier roots. Direct from the original Crazy Horse, the topless troupe at the MGM Grand puts on a sensuous show in a kaleidoscope of colors. MGM Grand Hotel. **702-891-7777**.

Jimmy's Naughty Nighty Night — Every July 12 at the Palms pool venue Skin there is a birthday celebration for Jimmy Tipton, the casino's director of player development. The event started as a VIP pajama party at the Hard Rock Hotel pool but relocated when Tipton moved to the Palms. Men usually show up in silk pajamas; women in unbelievable unmentionables. The private, invitation-only event has been featured on the E! Entertainment and Travel Channel cable networks.

Pimp 'n Ho Ball — You'll never see so many blushing beauties, most of them in panties and bras. Billed as the "biggest and baddest theme party," this sexified costume ball takes place every Labor Day weekend. Rock singer Pink was the Queen of Ceremonies for the 2003 ball at the Orleans Arena. 'N Sync's Lance Bass showed up in pimped-up purple with half-scale handcuffs as neckwear. The location varies year to year; see **www.spiritworld.com**.

Adult Video News awards program — Porn producers gather at the Venetian in January for the annual event that transforms the Sands Convention Center into an X-rated video bazaar out of Sodom and Gomorrah. If the Four Horsemen of Apocalypse ever ride into Las Vegas, figure this to be their first stop.

Rubber New Year's Ball — Remember the innocent old days, when we jammed Fremont Street by the thousands to see the fireworks launched off the roof of the Plaza hotel? That was kids' play. This one is another sexy costume party from the folks who bring you the Pimp 'n Ho. **www.spiritworld.com**.

Tangerine — Things have heated up at TI, formerly known as Treasure Island. Gone is the gun battle between pirates and the British naval gunboat HMS Britannia, replaced in 2003 by the *Sirens of TI*, or T & A, some suggest. The sexy transformation continued in the summer of 2004 when Tangerine Lounge & Nightclub, which overlooks the Sirens Cove, opened with Carmen Electra unveiling a new burlesque show. Dancers act out music ranging from "Big Spender," Jimmy Hendrix's "Light My Fire," to Outkast's "Hey Ya." TI. **702-894-7111**.

Zumanity — Cirque du Soleil's adult-themed show at New York-New York will shock the socks off most Middle American tourists with its edgy European-style content. It doesn't push the envelope, it shreds it. Don't say we didn't warn you. Rich-bitch sisters Paris and Nicky Hilton stormed out of the September 2003 premiere when edgy emcee Joey Arias, a New York drag diva, walked over and observed, "Clearly, this is the hooker section." New York-New York. **702-740-6969** or **866-606-7111**.

Pool options — Mandalay Bay's wave pool and Moorea Bay Club (topless), Bellagio, Caesars Palace, Venetian, Hard Rock and the Palms. (See Top 10 Hotel Pools, for descriptions.)

Golfing options —

Angel Park course, Monday - Thursday, $115-125; weekends, $125-145. **702-254-4653**.

Badlands Golf Club, Monday - Thursday, $135; weekends, $190. **702-363-0754**.

Las Vegas National Golf Club, Monday - Thursday, $125; weekends, $150. **702-796-0013**.

Legacy Golf Club, weekdays, $125; weekends, $145. **702-897-2187**.

Reflection Bay, Monday - Thursday, $235; weekends, $260. **702-740-4653**.

Lunch options — Olives patio at Bellagio, Mon Ami Gabi patio at Paris, Borders Grill at Mandalay Bay. Check the scores at ESPN Zone at New York-New York.

Pure fun options — Manhattan Express roller coaster at New York-New York, Big Shot at Stratosphere, Flyaway Indoor Skydiving, Fremont Street Experience, Wet N Wild water park.

Dinner options — N9NE at the Palms; Simon Kitchen & Bar at Hard Rock Hotel; Emeril's at MGM Grand; Delmonico at the Venetian; Morton's, Del Frisco's, Ruth's Chris Steak House, Spago at Forum Shops at Caesars; Ah Sin at Paris, adjacent to the nightclub Risqué.

Clubhopping — Club a Go Go offers a weekly clubbing tour and specializes in bachelor and bachelorette tours. Darva Conger went this route for her bachelorette party (no, not the one with Rick Rockwell). Private charters will pick you up at your hotel and stop at any three of these six properties: MGM Grand for Studio 54, Aladdin for Curve, the Rio for Club Rio, Venetian for C2K and Venus, Mandalay Bay for rumjungle and the House of Blues. **1-800-258-2218**. On-your-own options include the Hard Rock Hotel's center bar (be vigilant or you might run into you-know-who, in a veil and carrying one of those novelty penises), Rain at the Palms, Light at Bellagio, Coyote Ugly at New York-New York, Body English at Hard Rock Hotel, Studio 54 at MGM Grand, Tabu at MGM Grand, Curve at Aladdin. Tangerine at Treasure Island, OPM at Caesars, Risque at Paris, Bikinis at Rio and Zax at the Golden Nugget.

Strip club options — Sapphire, Jaguar, Club Paradise, Olympic Garden or **Vegasvip.com** (strippers to go.)

Sexy show options — *Zumanity* at New York-New York and *La Femme* at MGM Grand. Viewing options: ghostbar at the Palms, Voodoo Lounge at the Rio, Risqué at Paris; and, if you have juice, the House of Blues Foundation Room at Mandalay Bay.

Pool options — Mandalay Bay wave pool and Moorea Beach Club (topless), Bellagio, Caesars Palace, Venetian, Hard Rock and Palms.

Shopping options — Bellagio, Forum Shops at Caesars, Venetian, Fashion Show Mall (Neiman Marcus, Nordstrom, Macy's, and Tallulah G, for serious fashionistas).

Lunch options — Olives patio at Bellagio, Mon Ami Gabi patio at Paris, Borders Grill at Mandalay Bay, Mariposa at Neiman Marcus inside the Fashion Show Mall.

Pure fun options — Manhattan Express roller coaster at New York-New York, Big Shot ride at the Stratosphere, Flyaway Indoor Skydiving, bar hopping at the Fremont Street Experience, cooling off at Wet N Wild water park.

Salon and spa options — Canyon Ranch at the Venetian, Amp at Palms, Robert Cronin at Mandalay Bay, Salon at Bellagio (See Top Spas, for details).

Dinner options — Simon Kitchen & Bar at Hard Rock Hotel, N9NE at Palms, rumjungle at Mandalay Bay, China Grill at Mandalay Bay, Spago at the Forum Shops at Caesars, and Ah Sin at Paris Las Vegas (adjacent to the nightclub Risqué).

Clubhopping options — See the Bachelor list for the Club a Go Go tour option. On your own, the Hard Rock Hotel's center bar is a must for the bride-to-be rituals. There is also Rain at the Palms, Light at Bellagio, Body

English at the Hard Rock Hotel, Coyote Ugly at New York-New York, Studio 54 at MGM Grand, Tabu at MGM Grand and the House of Blues at Mandalay Bay. TI has burlesque shows at Tangerine.

Show options — *Zumanity* at New York-New York, *O* at Bellagio, *Mystère* at TI, *Mamma Mia!* at Mandalay Bay, or shopping humorist Rita Rudner at New York-New York. Male revues: *Chippendales: The Show at the Rio*; *Thunder From Down Under* at Excalibur.

View options — ghostbar at the Palms, Voodoo Lounge at the Rio; and, if you know the right people, the House of Blues Foundation Room at Mandalay Bay. And remember: What happens here, seldom stays here. It ends up in my column.

Chapter 4

Where to Eat

Long gone are the days of dirt-cheap midnight chuckwagon buffets and the trendy atom burgers (the original gut bombs?). Hollywood's chef to the stars Wolfgang Puck came along in the 1990s to lead a fine-dining revolution that sparked an unprecedented invasion of star chefs.

MOST ROMANTIC RESTAURANTS WITH VIEWS

February 'tis the season I get the most frequently-asked question about dining here: What are the most romantic restaurants for popping the question? My criteria is primarily influenced by the view, then the quality of the food and finally, the ambiance.

Alizé — Ask for one of the tables fronting the Las Vegas Strip at this penthouse gourmet room to experience one of the most dramatic views in the world. Palms. **702-951-7000**

Circo — Imagine Florence, but on the banks of the Seine, with a breathtaking view of the Eiffel Tower. Bellagio. **702-693-8150**

Eiffel Tower restaurant — At 11 stories up, it's the most dramatic view of the Bellagio's dancing fountains. Paris. **702-948-6937**

Japengo — The fine-dining gem overlooks Reflection Bay and a panoramic mountain backdrop. Worth the trip to the Hyatt Regency Lake Las Vegas Resort. 101 Montelago Blvd., Henderson. **702-567-1234**

Jasmine — Tom Cruise and Nicole spent time here during what was apparently their last getaway on December 28, 2000, before heading for Splitsville. Boffo Chinese Cantonese. Bellagio. **702-693-8166**

Le Cirque — The ultimate in over-the-top elegance and ambiance, plus that view of the Paris Hotel and its faux landmarks. Bellagio. **702-693-8100**

Panevino Ristorante — We have Tony Marnell Jr., the casino developer who created the Rio in 1990, to thank for this gem. It faces the southwest corner of McCarran International Airport, so it includes views of planes taking off and landing against the backdrop of the Strip, and gorgeous sunsets. There's even a train. Trains, planes, pastas and pizza — what more could one ask for? 246 Via Antonio. **702-222-2400**

Picasso — Start with $60 million worth of genuine Picassos on the walls, a priceless view of the dancing fountains outside, mix in an array of fresh flowers (reportedly $15,000 worth each month) and the ambiance of an Arabesque room. Viola! You have magic and chef Julian Serrano's superlative French Mediterranean cuisine. There's been many a proposal on the patio. The George Clooney-Julia Roberts dinner scene in *Ocean's Eleven* was shot here. Bellagio. **702-693-8105**

Prime — Welcome to what surely must be the world's most chichi steakhouse. And it only gets better at this Bellagio hotspot with its view of the dancing fountains and the dazzling features of the Eiffel Tower. Call ahead to reserve a window seat. Bellagio. **702-693-8484**

Top of the World Restaurant — One of the world's highest revolving restaurants, Top of the World has been a popular lovebird destination since the 110-story Stratosphere Tower opened in 1996. Stratosphere. **702-380-7711**

Alizé — The third and newest jewel in owner/chef Andre Rochat's fine-dining tiara — and the brightest. Located atop the Palms, Alizé offers one of the most spectacular panoramas of the Strip to go with its stunning menu. It was named one of Conde Naste's "75 top new restaurants in the world" (May 2003). The wine list offers 1,400 selections, plus Armagnacs, cognacs and ports. Palms. **702-951-7000**

Aureole — Chef Charlie Palmer's desert jewel is the home of the four-story wine tower that houses the world's largest wine vault (9,000 bottles). Small wonder it won *Wine Spectator's* most coveted award, the Grand Award, in 2001. Mandalay Bay. **702-632-7777**

Bradley Ogden — The ninth restaurant by the acclaimed Bay Area chef (does he ever sleep?) has one of the primo locations in the world. Maybe 50 feet away is the new $95 million, 4,000-seat Colosseum built by Caesars Palace for Celine Dion's three-year engagement. Ogden brings to Las Vegas the same touches that elevated 1 Market Street and Lark Creek Inn to San Francisco legend. In May 2004, Ogden was honored by the James Beard Foundation for "Best New Restaurant of the Year". Caesars Palace. **702-731-7110**

Commander's Palace — The famed New Orleans Brennan family joined the westward restaurant migration by bringing a version of their flagship eatery to Las Vegas in late 2000. With the move came such favorites as the sherry-flavored turtle soup, authentic Creole gumbo, the Louisiana pecan-crusted fish and the rave-worthy Creole bread pudding soufflé. Desert Passage at the Aladdin. **702-892-8272**

Le Cirque — The décor is as spectacular as chef Marc Poidevin's culinary mastery. That combination is why many diners rate it the ultimate Las Vegas dining experience. Some of the rarest wines in the world are among Le Cirque's selection: a 1961 Chateau Petrus fetches $17,295, a 1947 Chateau Cheval Blanc goes for $15,610, and a 1929 Musigny by Leroy is listed at $12,750. George Clooney dined here during the filming of *Ocean's Eleven*. New York City Mayor Rudolph Giuliani was warmly greeted by diners during a post-9/11 visit to Vegas. After former Secretary of Energy Bill Richardson had dinner with Michael Douglas and Catherine Zeta-Jones, the joke among the wait staff was that Richardson ordered his steak "nuked." Dress code: jackets and ties. Bellagio. **702-693-8100**

Michael's — In an effort to attract more high rollers to the Barbary Coast, Michael Gaughan added a gourmet restaurant in 1982 to build more buzz and business. For 20-plus years it has been pulling in big-name diners like Sharon Stone, Joe Pesci, Robert Redford, Michael Jordan, Jerry Lewis and No. 1 customer, Duke basketball coach Mike Krzyzewski. Maitre 'd Jose Martel's favorite memories: the night Pesci, in town to film *Casino*, revealed that long before his film career got off the ground he was a construction worker in Las Vegas; and super-shy Robert DiNiro asking Martel if he could enter through the kitchen on his next visit. The signature dish, sautéed Dover sole, goes for about $70 and it's criminal if you leave without trying the bananas foster or cherries jubilee. Barbary Coast. **702-737-7111**

Picasso — Most popular gourmet restaurant, best service and best décor: That's how Picasso and chef Julian Serrano fared in the 2001-2002 Zagat Survey. Two of the to-die-for items are the roasted day-boat diver scallops with potatoes mousseline and jus de veau, and the sautéed foie gras with Madeira sauce. Sightings include classical violinist Itzhak Perlman having Christmas Eve dinner in 2001 and actress Loni Anderson, stopping traffic in the kitchen. Bellagio. **702-693-7111**

Postrio — In 2000, The Venetian added Wolfgang Puck to its star chef lineup when he opened a more intimate same-named version of his by-the-bay eatery in San Francisco. John LaGrone, executive chef/associate partner of The Venetian, has an inspired menu with oceans of options, from white corn chowder with steamed manila clams, yukon potato, applewood smoked bacon, cilantro to pan seared John Dory, a regal white fish from the English Channel, and Moroccan-style eggplant with apricot cous cous. The Venetian. **702-414-1000**

Renoir — Talk about instant success. In less than two years after leaving the Phoenician hotel in Scottsdale, Arizona, chef Alessandro Stratta bagged two Mobil five-star awards for this luxurious French restaurant. Stratta developed his skills at Alain Ducasse's Louis XV restaurant in Monte Carlo. The Mirage. **702-791-7353**

Valentino — Luciano Pellegrini's father wanted him to follow in his footsteps as a stonemason in Bergamo, Italy, a city noted for opera and fine restaurants. Instead, Pellegrini followed his heart and wound up as executive chef at Valentino at The Venetian, earning a prestigious James Beard award for "Best Chef of the Southwest" in 2004. Maybe it was destiny, said Pellegrini. "Bergamo was the furthest outpost of the Venetian empire." Among his specialties: smoked roasted scallops, artichoke breaded John Dory filet, and cioppino Genoa style. The Venetian. **702-414-1000**

 ## TOP 10 OFF-STRIP RESTAURANTS

Andre's — Andre Rochat has been the most acclaimed chef in Las Vegas since launching his original Andre's French Restaurant downtown in 1980. He expanded to the Strip in 1997, opening Andre's at the Monte Carlo. It was voted the No. 1 restaurant in Las Vegas in Zagat's 2000-2001 restaurant guide, and ranked No. 3 in the 2001-2002 issue. Specialties include sautéed Muscovy duck breast, sauce Normandy with duck sausage and vegetable strudel, tornedos of veal medallions with Australian crayfish tails and sauce Choron, Chamonix potatoes, and asparagus tips Anglaise. Monte Carlo. **702-730-7777**

Hugo's Cellar — Another Old Vegas throwback. This downtown gem mixes charming traditions — a red rose to every female guest and the long-gone tableside salad cart — with classic cooking. You can figure the tab will be about $35 per entree. Four Queens Hotel, 202 Fremont St. **702-385-4011**

Lotus of Siam — "Best Thai restaurant in the country," proclaimed *Gourmet* magazine in 2001. That led to a visit by the Travel Channel and business has been boffo ever since for owner/chef Saipin Chutima and her husband Bill. Her catfish is so legendary that on one of my visits I saw a table of four first-time visitors order three versions of catfish and had rave reviews for each. The $8 lunch buffet is immensely popular. Caveat: Judge it not by the modest surroundings in the Commercial Center; it's all about the food. 953 E. Sahara Ave. **702-735-3033**

Mayflower — This was the birthplace of local fusion cooking long before the term went mainstream. Chef Ming See Woo's loyal followers include a number of "name" chefs who show up regularly for their fix. Don't be put off by the strip mall location; it's a local treasure. 4750 W. Sahara Ave. **702-870-8432**

Mimmo Ferraro's — Say "osso bucco" and Ferraro's pops up in many a local foodie's conversations. Julia Roberts loves the gnocchi; she dined here during the filming of *The Mexican* and *America's Sweetheart*. 5900 W. Flamingo Road. **702-364-5300**

Piero's Italian Cuisine — If these walls could talk. This site has a history dating back half a century. For almost 25 years it was the Villa d' Este, operated by Joe Pignatella and known for catering to a shiny and shady crowd. The Rat Pack and entourage were regulars. Mobster Tony Spilotro, who terrorized the town in the 1970s, preferred a table upstairs, out of public view. In the late 1980s Freddie Glusman bought the place and moved his Piero's restaurant from its location on Karen Street. Glusman brought over chef Gilbert Fetaz, former chef at Paul Anka's Jubilation. 355 Convention Center Drive. **702-369-2305**

Rosemary's — Serious foodies say it's a coin flip between Rosemary's and Mayflower as the best Off-Strip eatery. Owner/chefs Michael and Wendy Jordan have been packing the place since they set up shop at the West Sahara Promenade. Michael, a former top pupil of Emeril Lagasse, was executive chef at Emeril's New Orleans Fish House before going on his own. During their stay in New Orleans, Wendy worked with Chef Susan Spicer of Bayona and Chef John Neal of Peristyle. Their American cuisine includes Texas barbecue shrimp with Maytag blue cheese slaw, wild mushroom goat cheese gnocchi with chiffonade basil & roasted garlic sauce, roasted chestnut soup, and my favorite: pan-seared honey-glazed salmon with Granny Smith apple cabbage slaw, port wine syrup, candied walnuts and walnut vinaigrette. Rosemary's has won the *Las Vegas Review–Journal's* "Best of Las Vegas" categories for best gourmet restaurant, best desserts and place to impress a date. 8125 W. Sahara Ave. **702-869-2251**

Simon Kitchen & Bar — If you subscribe to the theory that food should be fun, you'll love the menu put together by chef Kerry Simon and restaurant partner Elizabeth Blau. It has all the staples, such as steak and salmon, meatloaf, beet salad, tandoori chicken, topless apple pie (hey, it's Vegas, baby), and maybe the world's most delicious banana bread. Did I mention the cotton candy? And let us not forget innovations like carpaccio pizza (seared beef, horseradish, roast tomatoes and arugula.) Simon's claims to fame: As a teen-ager, he worked at a Little Caesars pizza parlor in Evanston, Illinois, with an actor-to-be named Bill Murray. In April 2003, Simon was the centerfold in *Playgirl* magazine. Hard Rock Hotel, 4455 Paradise Road. **702-693-4444**

Spiedini Ristorante — Chef Gustav Mauler, who set up the kitchens at the Mirage, Treasure Island and Bellagio when they opened, named his place after the Italian style of skewer-cooking and offers a grilled spiedini of scallop and shrimp as a starter. Pastas are his passion and he delivers with Sinfonia di Mare (symphony of the sea): linguine with shrimp, scallops, asparagus, fresh tomatoes, lemon sauce; and fusilli with lobster, sun-dried tomato, baby peas and shiitake mushrooms, flamed with brandy in a rose cream sauce. J.W. Marriott, 221 N. Rampart Blvd. **702-869-8500**

Bon Jour Casual French Cafe — Marie and Bernard Calatayud had the good life going in Cannes, France. In 10 years they had built their La Cave restaurant into a hotspot that attracted the likes of Michael Douglas, Sharon Stone and Clint Eastwood during the Cannes Film Festival. But, said Bernard, "we are the kind of people who believe one life is not enough, so we decided to come to the U.S." They arrived in late 1999 and opened Bon Jour Casual French Cafe in early 2000. Marie, whose mother was a chef, makes a killer boulliabaise and crusted salmon in puff pastry with spinach, pine nuts and sour cream. 8878 S. Eastern Ave. Suite 100. **702-270-2102**

Binion's Horseshoe — The coffee shop is a historic breakfast stop for night owls, though hard times for the downtown casino seem to have finally put the legendary $2 (later $3) steak special to rest. Thank goodness there's still The Natural: two eggs, a huge ham steak, home-fried spuds, and toast for $4.99. ABC's late-night host Jimmy Kimmel claims he picked up his late-night habits here, capping many a night on the town as a teen-ager. Binion's. **702-382-1600**

Bootlegger Bistro — The closest thing to Old Vegas on the Strip, the Bootlegger is operated by Lt. Gov. Lorraine Hunt and her family. Solid Italian fare and one happening place on weekends, when a steady stream of headliners share the mic with Sinatra pally Sonny King. Live entertainment until 1 a.m. on most nights. Monday's karaoke with Kelly Clinton has caught on, thanks to regular appearances by Harrah's Clint Holmes, Bill Fayne, Holmes' musical director, and a host of local backup singers. Open 24 hours; breakfast starts at 11 p.m. 7700 Las Vegas Blvd. So. **702-736-4939**

Capozzoli's Ristorante —Capozzoli's is trapped in the 60s and you'll savor the experience as well as the homey Italian fare they serve until 4 a.m. on Fridays and Saturdays. Tom Jones is famous for popping in here and singing until dawn. When there isn't live music, there is a jukebox playing Frank and Dino. I would be remiss in not noting that because of a recent family tiff, Bobby Capozzoli opened Casa di Amore on East Tropicana and took along many of his business connections. 3333 S. Maryland Parkway. **702-731-5311**

Grand Lux — If you're not familiar with the name, and thus the concept, think Cheesecake Factory, with its monstrous portions and endless menu. The parent company went even bigger for this off-shoot at The Venetian. Pot roast is the house specialty and the caramel chicken is heavenly. Celebrities pour into this 24-7 eatery at all hours: New York Yankees manager Joe Torre is no stranger and the Osbournes — Ozzy, Sharon and brat pack — have made several visits. The Venetian. **702-414-1000**

Hamada — Jay Hamada took an improbable first step on his way to building a sushi empire. An appearance on the *Ed Sullivan Show*, with his dance troupe, started it all in 1959. After traveling the world, he eventually made his way back to Las Vegas where Kirk Kerkorian hired him to run the Benihana restaurant at his new International Hotel, now the Hilton. One night in the early 1970s daredevil Evel Knieval came in the restaurant. "He was my hero. He would come in with Elvis Presley." Thirty years later, Knievel still stops in to see his old friend, who started his restaurant chain in 1987. Hamada's has been a late-night institution ever since. On almost any night of the week, you'll spot booths full of Strip performers having post-show sushi at the new Flamingo spot, the busiest of five restaurant locations. Last seating is 3:30 a.m. 365 E. Flamingo Road. **702-733-3005** Other locations: Luxor, **702-262-4549**; Polo Towers, **702-736-1984**; Rio, **702-777-2770**; Stratosphere, **702-380-7766**; and Flamingo Hilton, **720-733-3455**.

Joyful House — Who is Yau Kai Wa? Possibly the best and busiest Asian chef in Las Vegas. By day, he prepares his authentic Hong Kong dishes at Joyful House. Then at 3 p.m., it's off to Pearl, the shining addition to MGM Grand's restaurant row where he's the executive chef. At 11 p.m., he heads back to Joyful House for the late shift and a crush of hungry late-arriving local chefs who are regulars — the ultimate sign of respect in the restaurant community. They also love it because it's open until 3 a.m. Recommendations: Peking duck, spicy stir-fried crab, mayonaise shrimp, and salt-and-pepper shrimp. 4601 Spring Mountain Road. **702-889-8881**

Malibu Chan's — This is a popular stop for the "show kids" who gather after their performances to pound sushi and brewskies. Some of the yummiest items include Cajun ahi pizza, portabella pizza and Asian salmon cakes. 8125 W. Sahara Ave. **702-312-4267**

Mr. Lucky's at the Hard Rock Hotel — Nothing dicey about this recommendation: Ask for the off-menu special at this 24-7 eatery. For $7.77 you get a steak, three broiled shrimp and a small mountain of garlic mashed potatoes. I took a party of six to dinner here one night, and the tab and tip didn't come to $100. Hard Rock Hotel, 4455 Paradise Road. **702-693-5000**

Peppermill Inn — Ah, the Peppermill, where many a night on the town has ended with flapjacks, eggs and strong coffee. They've been serving the late-night crowd here since December 26, 1972, and there's a 50-50 chance your server was among the original hash-slingers. During the filming of *Casino* in 1994, Sharon Stone, Robert De Niro and entourages took a liking to the fireside setting in the lounge. Many a Stardust showgirl has popped in here for a pre-show libation. Open 24-7. 2985 Las Vegas Blvd. South. **702-735-4177**

Ruth's Chris Steak House — A late-night menu after 10:30 p.m. brings in the after-show celeb crowd, including the likes of Ray Charles and *Everybody Loves Raymond* star Brad Garrett, who bellowed to owner Marcel Taylor: "Hey, Marcel! Nice restaurant, but next time could you get me a table near a waiter?" Most nights you'll find Taylor at his favorite table, working the house and downing a midnight steak. There's live music Thursdays through Saturdays, when things are hopping until 2:30 a.m. 4561 W. Flamingo Road. **702-248-7011**

 BEST BUFFETS AND BRUNCHES

The Buffet at Bellagio — A buffet as regal as the property, it ranks No. 1 or 2 every year in "best of" surveys. The best reasons to go are the lavish spread featuring king crab kegs, de-veined shrimp, Asian and Italian specialties, and a spectacular dessert spread with custard bread pudding, creamy rice pudding and peach cobbler (thoughtfully placed next to the self-serve soft ice cream machines). Bellagio. **702-693-7111**

Carnival World Buffet — On average, 5,000 pounds of crab legs and shrimp are consumed daily at the Rio's buffet by 7,000-to-11,000 diners every day. Food stations include: American, Chinese, Japanese, Italian, Mexican and fish

& chips, all for less than $20. The restaurant interior was recently renovated and now includes an amazing dessert bar and a VIP dining room. Saturday and Sunday brunches are from 8:30 a.m. to 3:30 p.m. Rio, 3700 W. Flamingo Road. **702-252-7777**

Green Valley Ranch Buffet — The Feast Around The World Buffet covers a lot of territory at a fair value (less than $20). Diners devour 20,000 pounds of Dungeness crab a month. The Saturday and Sunday brunches include free champagne and they go through 1,200 glasses of bubbly each day. Green Valley Ranch Station Casino, 2300 Paseo Verde Parkway, Henderson. **702-617-7777**

House of Blues Gospel Brunch — Between the great live music and an "all-you-can-eat" Southern-style brunch buffet, there's never a dull moment inside this nightclub lined with folk art. One day the gospel group found a new tambourine player in its ranks: actor Antonio Banderas, in town to film *Play It to The Bone*. Another time, Stevie Wonder walked out of the wings to sing "Happy Birthday" to a special guest. Sundays only; seatings at 10 a.m. and 1 p.m. Mandalay Bay. **702-632-7777**

Le Village Buffet — A gastronomical tour of five French provinces. Dinner includes bouillabaisse, lamb, venison, crab legs and prime rib. Desserts include bananas foster, crepes and crème brulee. Sunday's champagne brunch runs from 11:30 a.m. to 4:30 p.m. Paris Las Vegas. **702-946-7000**

Cravings — The Mirage unveiled in May 2004 its $12.5 million renovated buffet, an Adam Tihany-designed creation that he calls "an earthquake" in the buffet business. Tihany, a force in Las Vegas restaurant design, used many of his favorite elements to bring a less cavernous, more contemporary feel. Food preparation is more out in the open and the move toward smaller stations allows more frequent rotation to maintain freshness. One of the signature items is the cold strawberry soup. The corn chowder makes regular appearances, as does the chocolate bread pudding. The Mirage. **702-791- 7355**

Spice Market Buffet — Hands-down the best buffet value in town and many rate it in the top three, behind the Bellagio and Le Village at the Paris, for quality and selection. The Middle Eastern food station sets it apart from the city's many spreads. Plus, there's seafood, Italian, Asian and Mexican fare. Aladdin. **702-736-0111**

The Steak House at Circus Circus — Sunday's champagne brunch long reigned as the city's best, winning numerous "best of" surveys until the mega-resorts started emphasizing the big buffets. It's still an impressive spread. Seatings at 9:30 a.m.,11:30 a.m. and 1:30 p.m. Circus Circus. **702-734-0410**

Sterling Brunch — Elvis would have loved it because this is truly the king of buffets. You'll pay a princely sum — $52.95 at this writing — the top price in Vegas. A few reasons to justify the expense: all-you-can-drink Mumm Cordon Rouge champagne, broiled Maine lobster, Thai-marinated lamb rack, oysters and clams on the half shell, assorted sushi, lobster gazpacho, roast salmon in phyllo dough with shrimp spinach mousseline, chanterelles crusted beef tenderloin with roasted shallots and Pinot Noir au jus, and primo desserts. Offered only on Sunday from 9:30 a.m. to 2:30 p.m. Bally's. **702-739-4111**

Village Seafood Buffet — A daily seafood spread like no other in town; this one set the bar. Even at $30 it's a bargain, considering it offers lobster nightly on occasion: (two slipper tails and Maine) plus other international serving stations and hard-carved prime rib. A popular addition in 2003 was the lobster taco station. Never thought I'd ever say this in print, but the two-hour wait is worth it. Rio, 3700 W. Flamingo Road. **702-252-7777**

 TOP 10 STEAKHOUSES

Charlie Palmer Steak — A limited steak selection but what they do, they do exquisitely. Two examples are the 12-ounce New York steak and seared beef tenderloin. This room tucked inside the Four Seasons gets its share of votes for No. 1 in town. Four Seasons at Mandalay Bay. **702-632-5120**

Craftsteak — We've come a long way, baby, from the days when The Flame, Bob Taylor's Ranch House and the Golden Steer were basically the best beef outposts. Craftsteak takes the steakhouse experience to another level. You could make a case for Craftsteak as a Top 10 fine dining entry. MGM Grand Hotel. **702-891-7318**

Del Frisco's Double Eagle Steakhouse — I could go on and on about the steaks and sautéed mushrooms and au gratin potatos and . . . O.K, O.K. then, my favorite story: A party of six arrives. Two guys and four gals with major-league credentials. For starters they knocked down six shots of Hardy Perfection cognac at $725 a shot. Then it was dinner and wine, very expensive wine. The bill: $12,000. Before leaving, they ordered four bottles of Hardy Perfection to be delivered to a Bellagio suite. 3925 Paradise Road. **702-796-0063**

Delmonico Steakhouse — This popular destination is another Emeril Lagasse operation and it's topnotch. I saw John Ratzenberger, Cliff Clavin on *Cheers*, put away the popular bone-in ribeye and, while he was leaving, rib a table of beefeaters for chowing down "like ravenous dogs." The private room off the kitchen is the scene of an infamous Robin Leach and friends incident involving whipped cream. The Venetian. **702-414-3737**

Morton's of Chicago — A new location and a bigger room have made it the busiest Morton's steakhouse in the nation. Regulars include Tony Curtis and Tom Selleck. General manager Daniel Hurst passed along this Jerry Lewis gem: The King of Comedy was in one night to celebrate the 46th birthday of his son Scott, one of his six boys. Taking a linen napkin by both ends, Lewis placed a pat of butter in the middle and yanked the ends, catapulting the butter to the ceiling, where it usually sticks. Lewis said Queen Elizabeth even broke into a rare smile when he performed that one at a dinner in England. 400 E. Flamingo Road. **702-893-0703**

N9NE —Chicago owners Michael Morton and Scott DeGraff, best pals since age 9, teamed up with Palms owner George Maloof to turn the Vegas nightlife scene upside down in 2001. N9NE is one of the three components, working in conjunction with the Palms' two nightclubs, Rain and ghostbar. Chef Barry Dakake's bone-in ribeye with steak fries and truffle gnocchi is my recommendation. Palms. **702-933-9900**

The Palm — It's long been the envy of Vegas restaurateurs for its high volume, and figures to draw even more traffic from the nearby Celine Dion show. You'll see the local Who's Who crowd here, powering down steak and lobster or hanging at the bar. Forum Shops at Caesars. **702-732 -7256**

Prime Steakhouse — Food writer John Mariani ranks Prime among the top 12 independent steakhouses in the country (*Playboy*, September 2001). This is the steak emporium, but the seafood is top rate as well; a special nod to the Dover sole. Bellagio. **702-693-7111**

Smith & Wollensky's — A stand-alone Strip location offers the same quality and service as the New York institution, with big rooms for the corporate crowd. Trent Reznor, lead singer of Nine Inch Nails, scored huge PR points with the wait staff in June 2000. While pounding down a mondo ribeye, Reznor hit it off with the servers and left a lengthy list of comp tickets to the Nails' concert at Thomas & Mack. 3767 Las Vegas Blvd. South.. **702-862-4100**

Ruth's Chris Steak House — Marcel Taylor started the steakhouse rage in 1989 when he opened his first location on Paradise Road. In 1993, his second followed on West Flamingo Road. The latter is one of the liveliest late-night spots in town. When Bill Gates showed up at the Paradise Road location in 2003, his security staff was spotted on the restaurant roof. 3900 Paradise Road, **702-791-7011, 702**-4561, W. Flamingo Road, **702-248-7011**.

 SEAFOOD HEAVEN

Michael Mina Bellagio — (Formerly Aqua) is off the chart of decadence. You'll find foie gras all over the menu. "That's been our thing since San Francisco: fish and foie," said chef Mark LoRusso, who trained with Thomas Keller and Charlie Palmer. They even have a foie gras cart for tableside service. During the Chinese New Year more than a dozen of the 1½-pound roast foie gras have been sold in a day at close to $100 each. Every year like clockwork, a small Asian lady in her 60s shows up and orders a whole 20-ounce-plus roast for herself. Brad Pitt and George Clooney were in during the filming of *Ocean's Eleven*. Bobby Brown orders the 2½-pound lobster, and Anthony Hopkins is a fan of the large caviar parfait which is layers of smoked salmon, potato cake, egg mixture, lemon crème fraiche and a choice of seven caviar ranging from $70 to $150. Bellagio. **702-693-8199**

Bally's Sterling Brunch — This Sunday-only extravaganza is the perfect hedonistic experience that is Las Vegas. Forget that it's the priciest brunch in town. For $52.95 (at this writing), there's all-you-can-eat broiled Maine lobster, sushi, salmon, roulades of sole, shellfish, lobster ravioli, fresh smoked Nova Salmon with bagels, caviar with blinis and grilled swordfish. And that's just on the left side of the menu. Bally's. **702-739-4111**

Buzio's — The adventurous will love the special twists at this restaurant with its prominent oyster bar: sesame seed-crusted ahi tuna with spicy soy and wasabi, and the Chilean seabass with Jamaican marinade. Also, there's excellent bouillabaisse, cioppino and seafood gumbo. The oyster bar has about 10 shellfish selections. The Rio. **702-252-7697**

Emeril's New Orleans Fish House — Need to feed those Cajun and Creole cravings? Emeril's is the Holy Grail in my book. Signature dishes include Andouille-crusted redfish served on a bed of creamy grits with an oyster-artichoke cream sauce, barbecue shrimp and pan-roasted gulf snapper with steamed mussels and kalamata olives. The banana cream pie is one of my five favorite desserts in town. Consider yourself lucky if you can find a chair at the oyster bar. MGM Grand Hotel. **702-891-7374**

McCormick and Schmick's — A whale of a menu, with 28 to 32 seafood species available on most days. If four to six kinds of oysters isn't intriguing enough, combine that idea with the best happy hours in town: 3:30-to-6:30 p.m. and 9:30-to-11 p.m. Arissa Hill of *Real World* stops in for a lemonade vodka. 335 Hughes Center Drive. **702-836-9000**

Pho Kim Long — Walk through the door and it's like walking into an aquarium. There are fish tanks everywhere, stocked with lobster, red snapper and grouper. Technically, this former noodle shop is Vietnamese, but the place has become so popular it has separate Vietnamese and Chinese kitchens. Both are under the direction of Hong Kong chef Che Tim Kok, who opened Moongate at The Mirage. For starters, we had the best hot-and-sour soup outside of San Francisco. Longtime Asian casino host Ernie Cheung, who brings his high rollers here, ordered an array of winning dishes, including lobster with black bean sauce and the honey walnut shrimp with mayonnaise sauce. 4023 Spring Mountain Road. **702-220-3613**

Rosewood Grill — Home of massive lobsters, weighing from three to 15 pounds. The house record is a 21½-pound beast that cost more than $400 and fed six people. One customer always goes for a 10-pounder. I've heard a mixed grill of comments: Some swear by it while others swear it's a tourist trap. There's an extensive steak menu as well. 3763 Las Vegas Blvd. So. **702-792-9099**

Roy's — Roy Yamaguchi expanded his Euro-Asian restaurant empire to Las Vegas, first in suburban Summerlin then along East Flamingo Road's restaurant row. The best sellers: blackened island ahi with spicy soy mustard butter, roasted macadamia nut mahi-mahi with lobster butter sauce and herb Hawaiian opakapaka with teardrop tomato pistou and crispy elephant garlic. Roy's added a Hawaiian fusion twist on sushi in 2003. 8701 West Charleston Blvd., **702-838-3620**; and 620 E. Flamingo Road, **702-691-2053**.

The Tillerman — A favorite of locals and food critics for 25 years. Mark DeMartino bought out Tom Capp in 1997 and brought back longtime chef Miguel Magano, who had left for the Bellagio. The big seller: Alaskan King Crab legs, the favorite of boxing promoter Don King. Ten fresh fish appear on the menu every night. 2245 E. Flamingo Road. **702-731-4036**

Village Seafood Buffet —You like seafood? This is the place. But get there early because the lines are always long which means you may have to wait more than an hour. You'll find oysters on the half shell, snow crab, salmon, snapper, mahi-mahi, catfish and peel-and-eat shrimp (the selection can depend on what's available). Rio. **702-252-7777**

 ## SUSHI JOINTS

Cafe Wasabi Sushi Bar — This newcomer, a San Diego offshoot, quickly gained acceptance and it wasn't a case of beginner's luck. Executive chef Rick Giffen, regional executive chef for the China Grill group for almost two years, and Ernest Park, sushi chef at La Costa and executive corporate sushi chef of Hyatt Regency (which opened a dozen Japengos), teamed up in the kitchen to bring instant credibility in July 2002. True to the concept, there's even wasabi in the cheesecake. "Our big thing is we try to stay hip and cutting edge. Whatever is fun and in season, we try to incorporate into our menus," says Giffen. Think Asian-fusion tapas. 7365 W. Sahara Ave. **702-804-9652**

Hamada of Japan — The people's choice. *Zagat Restaurant Guide* has rated Hamada the top Japanese restaurant in Nevada and *Review-Journal* readers have voted it "Best of Las Vegas" for Japanese restaurants. The new location near the "restaurant row" of

East Flamingo Road is the mothership of the Hamada empire and pulls in a late crowd of Strip performers. 365 Hughes Center Drive, **702-650-6400**; Others are located in the Towers Flamingo Hotel, **702-733-3455**; Polo Plaza, **702-736-1984**; MGM Grand Hotel, **702-891-3016**; Luxor, **702-262-4549**; and the Stratosphere, **702-380-7766**

Japengo — *Zagat* calls it "the best sushi in the valley" and rates it a "10" for setting. The Lake Las Vegas location makes it one of the few restaurants in the valley where you can watch sailboats drifting across a mountainous backdrop. Hyatt Regency Lake Las Vegas. **702-567-1234**

Malibu Chan's — Terence Fong, formerly of Gatsby's and Osaka, joined chef/owner Kevin Martinez in 2003 to create a formidable team. Try the pan-seared miso yaki seabass with a sweet soy and beurre blanc sauce, and the St. Louis pork rib with wasabi, mashed potatos, Asian slaw and fried onion rings. 8125 W. Sahara Ave. **702-312-4267**

Nobu — As the popularity of sushi has grown so has Nobu's reputation as an extraordinary experience of fused flavors. A favorite celeb stop: One night I saw new live-ins Andre Agassi and Steffi Graf at the sushi bar, leaving a $100 tip for the chef, and across the room, baseball slugger Vinny Castilla. Hard Rock Hotel. **702-693-5090**

Osaka Japanese Bistro — What does this say about Osaka's sushi? When Steve Wynn opened the Bellagio, the sushi came from Osaka. "We made a million pieces, 10,000 to 25,000 a day, for the buffet for two months," recalled owner Gene Nakanishi. Word on the street has it that the deal was worth half-a-million. Not bad for a tiny Japanese restaurant that had little company in 1967 on Sahara Avenue, when it was still a dirt road. "Sahara only went to Decatur then. We were considered the boonies," said Nakanishi, whose father Sam and mother Iako weathered some lean years. "When we opened, nobody liked Japanese food. The only way we survived was because my father was a travel agent and brought in tours from Japan." The word of mouth remains strong today: "Every major celebrity from Japan has visited at least once," Nakanishi said. "Pat Morita (*Karate Kid*) comes in once a week." K-I fighter Bob Sapp, the former NFL player turned Japanese cult hero, kept his weight above 360 by devouring platters of sukiyaki, mountain taro potato, raw squid fermented in soy beans and grilled salmon during a visit in August 2003. 7511 W. Lake Mead Blvd., **702-869-9494**; **702**-4205 W. Sahara Ave., **702-876-4988**.

Little Buddha — From the moment you walk into Little Buddha, you are surrounded in Asian artistry and sensuality. But don't let the awe-inspiring décor and cool, club-like Asian music fool you: Little Buddha is serious sushi. The Leggy Blonde and I have become addicted to the Little Buddha Roll, Palms Roll, and George's Lobster Roll. Palms. **702-942-7778**

Roy's — This recent arrival introduced a Hawaiian fusion twist to its sushi in 2003 and the results were boffo. Try Roy's house roll with snow crab, dynamite-style salmon and avocado; and Lakanilau or snow crab and asparagus topped with filet mignon. All are complemented by in-house sauces created every day, lobster butter and kabayaki, an eel sauce. 8701 West Charleston Ave., **702-838 3620**; and 620 E. Flamingo Road, **702-691-2053**.

Shintaro — Among my top three sushi experiences ever, even though my introduction here was a server dropping a lobster roll at my feet. Heavenly stuff, but pricey. Bellagio. **702-693-7111**

Sushi Fever — A big following makes this one of the busiest sushi spots in town. I'm a big fan of the sushi boat for two; enough for two ravenous lumberjacks. Sake fans can select from 28 brands. 7986 W. Sahara Ave. **702-838-2927**

 **BEST ASIAN**

China Grill — Outstanding fusion fare in a trendy setting. My party of eight discovered a treasure trove of delights in the "classics:" Shanghai lobster prepared with ginger, curry and crispy spinach; and barbequed salmon. Or try the lamb spareribs, lobster pancakes and a heavenly rice pudding. Mandalay Bay. **702-632-7777**

Chinois — Another entry in Wolfgang Puck's Los Angeles-based culinary empire. Chef Scott Irestone, who opened Puck's Postrio at The Venetian, helms a kitchen that brings together a boatload of Far East flavors, fusing Chinese, Japanese and Korean with French and Indian. Signature dishes: Shanghai lobster, sizzling whole catfish, Cantonese duck, Chinois chicken salad and the immensely popular appetizer, tempura tuna sashimi. Pamela Anderson attracted a crowd during a dinner with friends. Dennis Rodman and Carmen Electra camped at the bar for half a day just before heading off to the Little Chapel of the Flowers on November 15, 1998. Forum Shops at Caesars. **702-737-9700**

Crustacean — The An Family's famous roast crab and garlic noodles were introduced to Las Vegas in 2003. Shortly after, one of the city's best-known chefs started telling friends, "This might be the best restaurant in town." The corn soup, crowned with crab, is as regal as the family line. Family matriarch Helene An is the great-granddaughter of the Vice-King of Vietnam and the youngest of 17 children of the Grand Advisor to the King. Helene spent most of her youth soaking up the skills of her family's three chefs: Chinese, French and Vietnamese. After launching Crustacean in San Francisco, the family made an even bigger splash in Beverly Hills in 1997. *Esquire* magazine listed Crustacean among its "Top Ten" restaurants. Demi Moore and Ashton Kutcher showed up at 2 a.m. for the fabled garlic noodles after the Shane Mosley-Oscar De La Hoya fight in September 2003. Aladdin. **702-650-0507**

Joyful House — Having heard so many raves, I expected a letdown when I finally tried it. I need not have worried. It more than lives up to all the hype. Those tour buses full of Europeans and Japanese speak volumes. The salt-and-pepper shrimp is a jaw-dropping classic. 4601 West Spring Mountain Road. **702-889-8881**

Kung Fu — Longtime Asian casino host Ernie Cheung ranks Kung Fu among the top three Asian restaurants in town. It didn't take long to see why. The night of my introduction, the kitchen was preparing giant garlic tiger prawns for 40 Asian high rollers the Bellagio was sending over. Thailand's Princess Ubomrut has dined here three times. Owner Chain Wong has been dishing out some of the city's most authentic Thai food since 1970, when he went to work as an assistant at Ah So in Caesars Palace. Nine years later he opened Kung Fu at Union Plaza. In 1993, he moved to his current address. Recommendations: Tom Yum, the Thai version of hot-and-sour soup, is a standout, along with the stuffed fried chicken wings, satay and a truly extraordinary pad Thai that surpasses Lotus of Siam. 3505 S. Valley View Blvd. **702-247-4120**

Lotus of Siam — The culinary artistry of Thailand at its glorious best is found at this modest hole-in-the-wall a few blocks east of the Sahara hotel. But I offer this word of warning from someone with a love of spicy food that's just shy of sadistic: If the dish says hot, back off several notches. Don't even think about eating those baby chili peppers. You'll thank me later. The soups are sensationally fresh and flavorful. Saipin Chutima and her husband Bill have created a classic menu for the adventurous. There's an excellent lunch buffet from 11:30 a.m. to 2:30 p.m. 953 E. Sahara Ave., E-5. **702-735-3033**

Nobu — In my book, Picasso is the No. 1 dining experience in town and Nobu is No. 2. Chef Nobu Matsuhisa gained his global reputation for introducing Peruvian influences into

Japanese fare after a three-year visit to Peru. In a coup, Peter Morton added the pricey Nobu to his restaurant lineup in 1999 and it was an immediate hit with the celebrity crowd. For an introduction, you can't do better than the slightly cooked white fish sashimi in olive oil, flavored with garlic, ginger and sesame seeds; or Nobu's version of tiradito which is a finely sliced red snapper with chili paste, cilantro and yuzu, a lemony Japanese fruit. For the less adventurous there are salmon, scallops and tempura. Hard Rock Hotel. **702-693-5090**

Pearl — Each time I leave this upscale Chinese eatery, I'm convinced I've had the ultimate in Chinese cuisine. Chef Yau Kai Wa has cooked for presidents: Bill Clinton loved the coconut shrimp, baked Chilean seabass and hot-and-sour soup. The Maine lobster dish is fit for royalty. MGM Grand Hotel. **702-891-7777**

Royal Star — Acclaimed Hong Kong chef Kevin Wu has put together what many consider to be the best Asian menu in town. There's killer dim sum as well. Wu's sister eatery, Ping Pang Pong at the Gold Coast, is easier on the pocketbook and reminds me of some of San Francisco's best hole-in-the-wall treasures. The Venetian. **702-414-1888**

808 — The name comes from Hawaii's area code and chef Jean-Marie Josselin's heavenly Pacific Rim menu covers a lot of territory. Try the deconstructed Ahi roll appetizer: ahi tartare atop sushi rice layers of avocado salad and crab cerviche, with white truffle dressing and avruga caviar. The potato-crusted Hawaiian snapper is the signature dish. Caesars Palace. **702-731-7110**

Border Grill — Mary Sue Milliken and Susan Feniger, better known as the Food Channel's *Too Hot Tamales*, put their upscale spin on Mexican food and it's sensational. Hot tip: On nights when Mandalay Bay's outdoor beach concerts are sold out, grab a table at the upstairs patio overlooking the wave pool and listen in. Mandalay Bay. **702-632-7403**

Dona Maria Tamales— The best tamales in town. Get one a la carte enchilada-style — with verde or Colorado sauce, chips and one of the city's best salsas — and spend $3 with tip. Add a beer and the tab is still under $6. 910 Las Vegas Blvd. South, **702-382-6538**; 3205 N. Tenaya Way, **702-656-1600**.

El Sombrero — The oldest restaurant extant in Las Vegas. It opened in 1950 and looks like a Juarez jailhouse. There have been only two cooks in its 50-plus years; Jose Aragon has been there 33 years. Get huevos for lunch or dinner, or the burrito enchilada-style. Accompany your meal with a bottle of pineapple Jarritos (Mexican soda). For dessert, there's natillas, Mexican vanilla pudding with raisins. 807 S. Main St. **702-382-9234**

Isla Mexican Kitchen & Tequila Bar — Acapulco native Richard Sandoval, a hit in New York and Denver with his "modern Mexican" cuisine, opened at TI, formerly Treasure Island, in the summer of 2004. Sandoval, who partnered with famed opera star Placido Domingo in New York at Pompano, was voted one of "The Best New Restaurants in America" by *Esquire* magazine and among "Best Chefs of 2003" in *New York* magazine. Tomayo in Denver, my old stomping grounds, is my favorite Mexican restaurant. Guacamole lovers will love Isla's custom-designed roving guacamole cart that offers different varieties of our favorite green delicacy, from classic to lobster with achiote passion fruit and serrano chiles. Mariena Mercer a 21-year-old six-foot-one blond is the official Tequila Goddess. Her specialty: the $99 Margarita. Open at 11 a.m., closes at 2 a.m. **702-894-7111**.

La Barca Seafood Restaurant — Mexican seafood comes with several twists at this favorite for local Latinos. It's famous for the fish tacos and whopper-sized shellfish cocktails. Your can of Tecate comes with a fresh little shrimp served on top. But it's only open Fridays through Sundays. 953 Sahara Ave. **702-657-9700**

Lindo Michoacan — This longtime locals' favorite on the East side is recovering from a 2002 Thanksgiving fire. Newlyweds Andre Agassi and Stefanie Graf showed up for a very informal wedding-night dinner four days before she gave birth to Jaden Gil Agassi, who was a bit premature. Maybe they should bottle the hot sauce for expectant mothers. Favorites include the jumbo stuffed shrimp with Monterey Jack, wrapped in bacon; and carnitas with steak sautéed in cognac, onions and mushrooms. 2655 E. Desert Inn Road. **702-735-6828**

Diego — After the closures of Mark Miller's Coyote Cafe and Ricardo's, the MGM Grand came back with Diego in the summer of 2004. Diego is located in the space previously occupied by Ricardo's. The concept: small sharing plates for an assortment of tapas, the Spanish appetizers. Expect to see grande-size entrees and a big tequila selection developed by Julio Bermejo, the only American knighted as a Tequila Master by the Mexican government. Other twists: a mobile salsa cart with six original varieties, frozen Margarita Popsicles and Tequila Sorbet Shooters. MGM Grand. **702-891-1111**

Pink Taco — World-class carnitas, margaritas and senoritas. And that's just for starters for the rock-'n-roll crowd that jams the joint. Menu highlights are the killer sweet-corn tamales, marinated carne asada, and the grilled salmon in a sweet and spicy honey-chipotle glaze with tomato and herbed salsa. Dessert options: Flan, fried ice cream and an intense warm chocolate brownie. Hard Rock Hotel, 4455 Paradise Road. **702-693-5000**

Taqueria Canonita — Alena Pyles, who co-hosted the nationally syndicated public broadcasting series *New Tastes From Texas*, with brother and acclaimed southwestern chef Stephan Pyles, opened Taqueria Canonita in 1999 but recently moved on after four years. The salsas are primo and the vast menu includes six kinds of tacos, creative quesadillas, empanadas and clayudas (tortilla pizzas), plus platters of barbecued pork, spit-roasted chicken and grilled shrimp. Desserts include sweet potato flan, Margarita mousse, Mexican chocolate cake and fried bananas. The Venetian. **702-414-1000**

Viva Mercados — Owner Bobby Mercado spent 15 years at Viva Zapata, most of it developing the menu, before heading out on his own in 1980. His signature dishes, he says, are the chile relleno, lobster fajitas and Tilapia, a delicate white fish. I went for the parrillaea, the biggest platter of fajitas this side of the Rio Grande. "That's our true-blue fajitas dish with chicken, New York steak and pork, over sizzling onions," he said. For lovers of Mexican seafood there's mariscos parallaba, a sizzling skillet full of orange roughy, shrimp, langostinos and scallops. 6182 W. Flamingo Road. **702-871-8826**

 BEST ITALIAN

In the land of Sinatra and Spilotro, how could we confine this category to just 10?

Bella Luna — Marco Porceddu earned boy wonder status when, at age 25, he was hired by Steve Wynn as executive chef at Francesco's at Treasure Island. The skilled Sardinian had arrived in two years earlier, quickly making a name for himself as a sous chef at the Desert Inn's Portofino and the MGM Grand's Trevisi and La Scala restaurants. After leaving Francesco's in early 2003 to do consulting work for the Fertitta's Station Casinos, he found a new home at Bella Luna in late 2003. His speciality: provincial Italian cuisine, with an emphasis on risottos and imported Mediterrean fish. Opens at 5 p.m. Bella Luna. **702-227-7900**

Fellini's — This upscale, happening hangout offers heaping platters of Tuscan-style specialties and a piano bar that attracts legendary voices. 5555 West Charleston Blvd. **702-870-9999**. There is a second location at the Stratosphere. **702-380-7777**

Francesco's — New chef Edwin Pocasangre, Porceddu's successor, has kept the standards high and the menu happening. The Wynns continue to be regulars; Elaine's nuts over the Chilean seabass with grape sauce, I'm told. GM Steve Mainini and waiter Jan Bouziden are top notch. Tl. **702-894-7111**

Gaetano's Ristorante — Sicilian-born Gaetano Palmeri built a solid name in the Los Angeles area, then brought his family operation to Henderson for the new millennium and the word is out: This is a shining star. 10271 S. Eastern Ave., Henderson. **702-361-1661**

La Scala Ristorante Italiano — Don't let the off-Strip location, a long gnocchi throw from the Las Vegas Convention Center, fool you. This gem was previously on the MGM Grand's restaurant row before owner Roberto Perotti moved to Mark IV Tower on East Desert Inn Road. *Gourmet* magazine ranked it among its 2002 "neighborhood gems," one of only seven local eateries rating a mention. Lunch is one of the best deals in town. 1020 E. Desert Inn Road. **702-699-9980**

Osteria del Circo — Rated by most local food critics as the No. 1 Italian restaurant in town. It's another case of Steve Wynn talking the best into moving to the desert. Le Cirque patriarch Sirio Maccioni sent his sons to Las Vegas in 1999 and the rest is fine-dining history. Bellagio. **702-693-7111**

Pasta Shop & Ristorante — This intimate Italian jewel brought to you by David and Glen Alenik, serves the freshest pasta in town. Chef David had created some truly amazing sauces that capture the essence of true Italian cuisine. He has cooked his classic pasta for many Las Vegas legends, from Frank Sinatra to mobster Tony Spilotro. 2495 E. Tropicana Ave. **702-451-1893**

Piero's Italian Cuisine — Owner Fred Glusman turned Piero's into a Vegas version of what Ciro's was to another Hollywood era. The food is top-shelf and it's been one of the most popular celebrity hangouts for years, long before Sharon Stone shot *Casino* scenes inside. The back bar is a shrine to Glusman's pal, Jerry Tarkanian, the UNLV coaching icon. George Clooney was a regular during filming of the *Ocean's Eleven* remake and Jerry Lewis has his own table. Glusman let me know on my first visit that some politicians, talking deals in booths behind me, wouldn't appreciate being seen together in my "sightings." Put another way: What you see here, stays here. 355 Convention Center Drive. **702-369-2305**

Spiedini Ristorante — Austrian native Gustav Mauler has been dazzling local diners since 1987 and this is his pride and joy. He'll be even more involved now that he's turned Oxo, a sister venture only 30 feet away, into a nightclub called the Plush Lounge in a deal with the Key Club of Los Angeles. Ask for a recommendation and hear him rave about the salmon over corn and potato risotto. It's definitely worth a drive to suburban Summerlin. J.W. Marriott, 221 N. Rampart Blvd. **702-869-8500**

Stefano's — Set in a beautiful and romantic room, Stefano's is a gem that will not disappoint. The Cioppino is their most famous dish. I recommend the shrimp appetizer and the pasta bolognaise. And it is impossible to take just one bite of the tiramisu. In June 2004, most of the *Sopranos* cast in a scene that looked straight out of the show, dined at the restaurant and were serenaded by singing waiters. Stefano's is named after Vegas' most famous "Steve" – Steve Wynn. Wynn, former owner of the Golden Nugget, told the new owners that if they had other plans for Stefano's, he was interested in buying back the name. Golden Nugget. **702-385-7111**

Valentino — Chef-partner Luciano Pellegrini, a master of Northern Italian cuisine, teamed up with owner Piero Selvaggio, whose Valentino of Los Angeles has been frequently mentioned among America's top 10 restaurants and top three Italian eateries. The wine list is one of the most impressive anywhere, with 20,000 bottles. Best seat in the place: the wine cellar! Next best: Luciano's own chef table for eight in a private room, featuring a window view into the kitchen. The Venetian. **702-414-3000**

Ventano Corner Italian & Oyster Bar — Arnauld Briand started at the top when he arrived in the United States in 1984. Recruited from France by legendary New York restaurant developer Joe Baum, Briand was hired to raise the profile of the Windows of the World gourmet room atop the World Trade Center. His first job in Las Vegas was just as prestigious: He was executive chef of the Palace Court at Caesars Palace for five years, starting in 1990. There were stops at the Rainbow Room in New York and the Desert Inn in Vegas before he teamed up with partner Carmine Vento to open Ventano on December 12, 2002. "The day we opened we did 30 covers and five days later we were doing 350. And we're in Henderson," Briand noted. Many come for the signature appetizer:

a shrimp marinated in olive oil, garlic and chili pepper, served on a 700-degree rectangle of granite and sprinkled with lime. Briand's osso bucco features lamb instead of veal. And his crème brulee has been "the best in the U.S. for 10 years," he says. 191 Arroyo Grande Blvd. **702-944-4848**

Zefferino — Chef Francesco Schintu was the right-hand man in Genoa to original chef Gian Paolo Belloni, perhaps the only chef who has cooked for both the Pope and Frank Sinatra. The brunch is among the best on the Strip and I had a memorable Christmas feast featuring lobster tails and the legendary dish of sautéed veal with anchovy-accented tuna sauce. The Venetian. **702-414-1000**

 PIZZA PIE TO DIE FOR

Beach Pizza — Owner Larry Getzoff first cultivated a following among L.A.'s beach communities and now he's carving out a beachhead in Las Vegas. Beach Pizza has been named among *Pizza Today* trade magazine's "Hot Pizzerias" four years in a row, and was a winner of Best Pizza by readers of a Los Angeles entertainment guide. Tiger Woods has been known to stop in at the Manhattan Beach store; Sting dined there with his limo parked outside. And "we delivered pizza to the Stones' private jet at LAX," Getzoff says. Recommended: the garlicky scampi pizza and the barbecued chicken. 1780 N. Buffalo Drive. **702-255-8646**

Fasolini's Pizza Café — Owner Jimmy Fasolini and his wife Josie brought their Philadelphia recipes with them. This restaurant in a Target parking lot has been a favorite stop of Siegfried and Roy, Jerry Lewis, Debbie Reynolds, Marty Allen and Dom DeLuise. If he's not too busy, ask Jimmy to show you the hairpiece Frank Sinatra wore when he played Caesars Palace in 1974. 222 S. Decatur Blvd. **702-877-007**.

Il Fornaio — Five-star stuff, including what I'd humbly submit as the pizza "find" of the year: the Capricciosa, loaded with prosciutto cotto, mushrooms, kalamata olives, artichokes, mozzarella cheese and oregano. I had to fend off Coyote Ugly co-owner Jen Worthington for the scraps. New York-New York. **702-650-6500**

Papreza's — Jimmy Pieprzyca moved to Las Vegas from Chicago in 2001 to help open Palms nightclub Rain as assistant general manager. He also brought his passion for Chicago-style pizza, having operated a string of Rosati's in the Chicago area. Addicts of deep-dish pies will be in heaven. The "Full House" is highly recommended as a hangover cure, so they tell me. 9770 S. Maryland Parkway. **702-407-7575**

Pizzeria Regina — Boston's top-ranked pizza in many Beantown readership polls. Palms owner George Maloof lured the franchise west after living on Pizzeria Regina pies during his prep school days at Phillips Andover. Palms. **702-942-7777**

Rocco's New York Italian Deli Pizzeria — As advertised, the real-deal New York pie. Brooklynese is spoken here; you should hear the steady stream of transplants who come in for take-out. Not a lot of tables, but who cares? The TV is always on one of the New

York stations via satellite feed. 1181 S. Buffalo Drive. **702-254-4777**

Nick & Tony's — The pepperoni pizza at Nick & Tony's, formerly the space occupied by Sammy's Woodfired Pizza, is a guaranteed slice of heaven. Co-owner Nick Bimonte, formerly owned Nick's on the Strip. 3900 Paradise Road. **702-836-1999**

Spago — Puck's celebrity pizzas became the rage in Hollywood, especially the signature pie: smoked salmon, thin-sliced onions, chives, dill cream and sevruga caviar, a fixture at the Oscar parties he caters. The Forum Shops at Caesars. **702-369-0360**

Trattoria del Lupo — It's one of three Wolfgang Puck restaurants on this list, and there's a reason: When it comes to pizza, the guy brings it all to the table. My favorites: meatballs, provolone and shaved white onions; and the basil pesto version with sun-dried tomatoes and pine nuts. Mandalay Bay. **702-632-7777**

Wolfgang Puck Bar & Grill — A name change from Wolfgang Puck Cafe was just the beginning when the new look was unveiled in June 2004. A major renovation positioned Puck for the tidal wave that's expected when the new Cirque du Soleil opens nearby at the MGM Grand. The menu changed too, but Puck's designer pizzas are a constant. Some of the winners: wild mushrooms, leeks, thyme and goat cheese; Italian sausage with sweet onions and oregano; garlic chicken, roasted peppers and parsley; pesto shrimp, artichokes, sun-dried tomatoes, and the ham calzone with four cheeses. MGM Grand. **702-891-3000**

Chapter 5

Entertainment Today

The closure of Siegfried and Roy's show in October 2003 left a big question: With the famed duo no longer one of the Strip's main attractions after a 13-year, 30,000-performance run at the Mirage, who fills the void? Phantom of the Opera? We Will Rock You? Or the latest newcomer from Cirque du Soleil? Without Sigfried and Roy, Las Vegas is closer to becoming Cirque City.

Blue Man Group: Live at Luxor — This show rocks — seriously, with an electrified band rarely found in standing shows on the Strip — and the energetic rhythms help draw both baby boomers and teens to the "Blue" humor of three silent, skullcapped pranksters. It's street theater meets weird science project, set to a spacey spaghetti Western soundtrack. Luxor. **702-262-4400**

Celine Dion: A New Day... — The most talked-about entertainment development on the Strip does capacity business even as it inspires debate about whether the Canadian songstress found a thematic fit in the baroque visions of former Cirque du Soleil director Franco Dragone. Celine fans are likely to revel in every nuance and note, though some may agree with my opening-night impression that it's too super-sized; the pop superstar is often lost against the giant screen and vast stage. Caesars Palace. **702-731-7865**

Danny Gans — Impressionists were left behind with the variety era until this athletic young performer revived the genre and made it appeal to a new generation. Audiences marvel at Gans' vocal genius in duplicating 60-plus voices in 90 minutes. His duet — yes, duet — of Nat King Cole and Natalie is a showstopper. The Mirage. **702-791-7111**

Clint Holmes — His father was a black jazz singer; his mother a British opera singer. It figured the gene pool would produce a special performer. Holmes only hit, "Playground in My

Mind," reached No. 1 in 1974, but doesn't reflect what he does these days. He performs in a Harrah's showroom that Sammy Davis Jr. opened and, like Sammy, leaves it all on stage, night after night. Harrah's. **702-369-5111**

Gladys Knight — This Rock & Roll Hall of Famer and R&B queen could fill up more than one show with her prodigious list of hits, but she also remembers to broaden the scope of her Las Vegas show. Knight has lived in Las Vegas for years, but grew weary of the road in 2002. Her enthusiasm for working close to home lights up the stage. Flamingo. **702-733-3333**

Mamma Mia! — It's worked everywhere else, so why not Vegas? Take the music of ABBA, the disco-pop hitmakers of the '70s, add a love story with more twisty-turns than Greece's shoreline and you've got a feel-good show that allows baby boomers to understand how characters in those old Broadway musicals could suddenly just break into song. Mandalay Bay. **702-632-7580**

Mystère — This was Cirque du Soleil's first roll of the dice for a permanent show on the Strip. Who knew it was the beachhead that allowed the Canadian company to take over Las Vegas, with three shows on the Strip and another on the way? A lot of people still like it better than either *O* or *Zumanity*. TI. **702-392-1999**

O — An otherworldly waking dream performed in, over and on water by Cirque du Soleil. The liquid stage turns to dry land and back again in moments. It remains the pinnacle of customized construction that demonstrates what the Strip can do like no other place: Create one-of-a-kind shows that are physically impossible to tour. Bellagio. **702-693-7722**

Elton John — The critics loved it from the minute this rocket left the launching pad. "The Colosseum may be known as the house that Dion built, but the ambition and artistry of John's show is what gives the room its first 'must see,' " wrote Robert Hilburn of the *Los Angeles Times*. *USA Today* gave the John-David LaChapelle collaboration four stars, the ultimate, saying *The Red Piano* is "too stately a title for this eye-popping, jaw-dropping spree." In no time, extra dates were added to John's original deal for 75 shows over three years. Caesars Palace. **702-731-7110**

Zumanity — Cirque du Soleil tried not to repeat its other two Las Vegas shows, and so turned to the very-Las Vegas theme of sex for a show that attempted to be a bawdy update of European cabaret. The redressed — or, much of the time, undressed — acrobatic routines achieve great moments of beauty and sensuality. But other elements were uneven or simply crude when the show opened in August 2003. New York-New York. **702-740-6969**

 TOP 10 FUNNIEST SHOWS

The Amazing Jonathan — Gut-busting magician-gone-bad shtick creates the funniest show on the Strip. Johnathan's dim-bulb sidekick, "Psychic Tanya," (Penny Wiggins) gets this vote for the Strip's Best Supporting Actress. Don't even think about bringing the youngsters. Riviera. **702-734-5110**

Blue Man Group: Live At Luxor — Delightfully inventive without saying a word, they take g-rated humor to a unique place that mixes junior-high cafeteria stunts with thoughtful social insights. The biggest laughs come from the former and involve Cap'n Crunch cereal, marshmallows and, in one of the most hilarious segments on the Strip, Twinkies and a hapless female volunteer. Luxor. **702-262-4400**

Beacher's Madhouse — Creator/host Jeff Beacher created a splash even before bringing his zany troupe from Broadway to Las Vegas in December 2003. The beefy Beacher dressed up as a maintenance man, threw a ladder over his shoulder and walked into the MGM Grand, where he stripped to a Speedo and dove into a large fish tank at the Rainforest Cafe. His first show at the Hard Rock Hotel was even wilder: "It was 'Studio 54' meets *Kings of Comedy*, meets *Jackass*, meets *Girls Gone Wild*." Oh, yes, and there's 65 female dancers on 15 stages and 20 variety acts. Most Saturday nights in The Joint. Hard Rock Hotel. **702-693-5000**

An Evening at La Cage — Frank Marino as Joan Rivers heads this talented cast of female impersonators who salute most of the first-name-only strata of divas, from Bette to Barbra, Tina to Cher. Riviera. **702-794-9433**

George Wallace — Looking for a late show? George Wallace's 10 p.m. act is a laugh riot with his rapid-fire observational humor. On Wallace's opening night at the Flamingo in January 2004, his ex-roomie Jerry Seinfeld did a 10-minute walk-on. Wallace is known to hand over a c-note to audience members and have them run out into the casino and try their luck. Flamingo. **702-733-3111**

Penn & Teller — This odd-couple team got its reputation as "Bad Boys of Magic" by exposing older tricks of the trade. And it's a hoot to watch them do it as Penn Jillette, the big guy, pontificates and deconstructs while Teller silently acts out the exposé. They finish with a bang by catching .357-magnum bullets in their teeth. Magic with an edge. Rio, 3700 W. Flamingo Road. **702-777-7776**

Rita Rudner — The queen of shopping one-liners became a resident headliner at New York-New York in 2001 and celebrated her 1,000th performance in the summer of 2004. The author of *Rita Rudner's Guide to Men* and *Tickled Pink*, she's a must for bachelorette parties. New York, New York. **702-640-6969**

The Scintas — This legendary musical family from Buffalo, New York, is a throwback to TV's variety era. Joe Scinta's impression of Joe Cocker is the best since John Belushi's and should be in the Impersonators Hall of Fame. It was so gut-busting, literally, that he had to table it for a time due to hernia problems. The Rio, 3700 W. Flamingo Road. **702-777-7776**

The Second City — The Chicago troupe that created the *Saturday Night Live* style of ensemble humor now brings sketch comedy and improvisations to the Strip. Cast members Jason Sudeikis and Kay Cannon returned to Chicago during a break and came back engaged. Sudeikis — nephew of *Cheers* star George Wendt (the other Norm) — and fellow cast member Seamus McCarthy were invited to audition for *Saturday Night Live* in

August 2003, and Sudeikis was hired as a writer. Flamingo. **702-733-3333**

Downtown Gordie Brown — When the new owners Tim Poster and Tom Breitling took over the Golden Nugget, one of their first moves was to hired Brown, who had polished his impersonation show in Reno, as their resident headliner. Brown was a 20-something political cartoonist in Canada at the *Ottawa Sunday Herald* when he attended a performance by Rich Little, who grew up in Ottawa. "That was it for me. I wanted to be that man," said Brown. Little, a Las Vegas resident, was in the audience the night of Brown's headliner debut. "He's grown so much. He's doing voices never done before," said Little. The Golden Nugget. **702-385-7111**

 BEST LOUNGE SHOWS

Bobby Barrett — This former Boston postal worker got tired of hearing how much his voice sounded like 'Ol Blue Eyes and decided to do something about it. He landed his first big gig as a Frank Sinatra sound-alike here on May 14, 1998, the night Sinatra died. (Barrett doesn't have a permanent berth at any one casino so e-mail him to get his schedule: **artanis97@aol.com**.)

The Bootlegger Bistro — Lt. Gov. Lorraine Hunt and her family moved to the south end of Las Vegas Boulevard in late 2000 and their fans followed. Sonny King, a Sinatra pal and longtime local lounge legend, stills holds forth on weekends, often pairing up with Old Vegas legends and current headliners who show up after their shows. Monday nights are a hoot, with karaoke queen Kelly Clinton joined by a succession of local stars. If you're lucky enough to find a seat, order up some Italian. 7700 Las Vegas Blvd. S. **702-736-4939**

Paragon — When Jimmy Hopper left the Bellagio's Fontana Room in early 2004 to expand his horizons, the void in the lounge scene was palpable. Enter the unique sounds of Paragon, a symphonic rock band featuring a nine-member group, including four rhythm players and four string players. Tuesday - Thursday, 9:30 - 1 a.m.; Friday - Saturday, 6:30 -10 p.m. Bellagio. **702-693-7111**

David Osborne — This pianist extraordinaire has performed for presidents Jimmy Carter, Ronald Reagan, George Bush and Bill Clinton. He sells tons of CDs but not in record stores. The next time you are in a collectibles shop, listen carefully and look for his CDs on display. Café Lago, Caesars Palace. **702-731-7110**

The Lon Bronson All-Star Band — A longtime fixture at the Riviera's Le Bistro Lounge, Bronson and friends relocated to the Golden Nugget in the Summer of 2004. Because they play at midnight on Saturday and 10 p.m. Mondays, Bronson's 13-member group is made up of top musicians either moonlighting or working on a night off. Two-drink minimum. The Golden Nugget. **702-385-7111**

Cook E. Jarr — We're not woofin' on this pick. Late-night crowds have been been diggin' Jarr's throwback act for 20 years. When he's not barking up business for Harrah's Carnaval Court on Tuesdays and Wednesdays, 11 p.m. - 1 a.m., he's running with his pals Tom

Jones and Bill Medley. See you there, dawg. Harrah's. **702-369-5000**

Louie Louie — Another campy, fashion-disaster singer with a dynamic show and big local following. Catch him at The Show Bar Lounge at the MGM Grand on Saturdays and Sundays. He had a top 20 *Billboard* hit "Sittin' in the Lap of Luxury" and was Madonna's leading man in her *Borderline* video. MGM Grand. **702-891-1111**

Napoleon's — An elegant room (if you don't mind cigar smoke), featuring elegant jazz by local saxophone fixture Tommy Thompson. Paris Las Vegas. **702-946-7000**

The Tribute to Frank, Sammy, Joey and Dean — Technically not a lounge show, but a must-see for those who want a lesson in why the Rat Pack's lounge roosts lasted all night. Co-producer Sandy Hackett, son of the late Buddy Hackett, also does a terrific Joey Bishop. Greek Isles Hotel, 305 Convention Center Drive. **702-952-8000**

Marlene Ricci — This versatile cabaret singer's career was launched in the late 1970s, when Frank Sinatra was talked into watching a set at the Aladdin and was so impressed that he took her on the road as an opening act for two years. Riviera. **702-794-9433**

 ## THE ELITE ELVI: THE BEST OF THE ELVIS IMPERSONATORS

Jim LeBoeuf — A beefy Elvis who prioritizes fun over accuracy, LeBoeuf was a fixture at the Riviera for years until the hotel started cutting corners on its budget. "Great presentation," says a fellow Elvi. He appeared in *3,000 Miles to Graceland* — along with many others listed here — but don't hold that against him. For updates on his current whereabouts, check **www.jimaselvis.com**.

Trent Carlini — Carlini was named "Best Elvis Performer in the World" in a 1996 competiton in Montreal. He prefers to be characterized as an Elvis "stylist" as opposed to "impersonator." By whatever definition, his five-year run in *Legends in Concert* at the Imperial Palace paved the way for a shot at the real Elvis stage of the Las Vegas Hilton's showroom. He outdrew many real-deal performers such as Sheena Easton and the Smothers Brothers, and was rewarded with more weeks at the Hilton in 2004. One of his competitors says Carlini "goes from the different Elvis looks better than anyone." Hunky, toned and talented, he's Elvis in the "pre-love handles" era.

Steve Connolly — "The Black Leather Elvis" polished his act in the Boston area and moved here in 1996. "I did 70 shows a year my last year in Boston. My first year here I did 700 as a newcomer," thanks to lounge and theme park work. Connolly resides in the posh Southern Highland residential development, where Reggie Jackson bought three homes, so it's safe to say this Elvis is in the chips. In the summer of 2003 he accepted an open-ended stint at Fitzgeralds downtown.

Jesse Garon — Elvis buffs will recognize the first and middle name of Presley's stillborn twin brother. Others may recognize him from the November 1998 cover of *Time* magazine, next to his neon-lit 1955 pink Fleetwood Cadillac. He is considered to be among the top five revenue-producing Elvises. He has no permanent showcase on the Strip, so track him down at **www.vegaselvis.com**.

Darren Lee — This Canadian native went to Memphis on the 20th anniversary of Elvis' death and finished first among 397 Elvis contest performers. He's a star of the Stratosphere's *American Superstars*. His rendition of "I'm Hurt" is so good it hurts.

Matt Lewis — The new legend of the Imperial Palace's *Legends in Concert* (the Presley finale is the one constant in the otherwise rotating lineup) replaced Grahame Patrick in April 2003 when the latter ended a six-year run to take a job in Berlin.

Greg Miller — Another *Legends in Concert* graduate is now well entrenched in the corporate world. Translation: He's pulling in big bucks, which, I'm told, range from $75,000 per year to $300,000 for the upper echelon Elvi. Find him through **www.elvisinvegas.net**.

Brendan Paul — One of the tallest Elvises at six-foot-four, he also did a *Legends in Concert* stint before becoming one of the most-booked corporate Elvis acts in the country. Find him through **www.classique-productions.com**.

James Rompel — Another *Legends in Concert* alumnus now stars in *Early Elvis*. He's portrayed Elvis in TV biographies, MTV videos and AT&T commercials. E-mail him at **acimforpeace@usa.net**.

Pete Willcox — "He's the Babe Ruth of Elvi," says Connolly. Even Elvis was impressed. "When Fonz hits the jukebox in *Happy Days* and Elvis' "Hound Dog" starts playing, that's my voice. Elvis told me he thought it was his voice," says Willcox, who caught fire in the early 1980s and became the darling of TV, landing on *Cheers, Designing Women, L.A. Law, Murphy Brown, Alf, ER*, and *Full House*. He's so versatile that he's now playing Dino in *The Tribute to Frank, Sammy, Joey and Dean* at the Greek Isles. For Elvis gigs, check **www.worldsgreatestelvis.com**.

EVERYTHING ELVIS

The Elvis Extravaganza Impersonator Contest is an annual three-day event each January at the Westward Ho. The rest of the year, Las Vegas booking agents have Elvi for all occasions — and we mean all occasions. Here are some of the options.

All-Elvis Choir — The visual, I'm told, is "off the charts." Choir members come from a pool of about 20 top Elvis impersonators. Contact: Always Entertaining. **702-737-3232**

"Big Elvis" — Weighing in at more than 500 pounds, Pete Vallee is one humongous hunk of burnin' love, so don't expect any karate kicks. This Barbary Coast lounge attraction thinks his mother isn't telling him everything. He had a DNA test because his late father Claude "didn't think I was his kid," and his mother was a singer in Nashville when Elvis worked there in the '60s. The results didn't turn the Graceland legal department on its ears. Contact: Tom Star. **702-563-2793**

The 40-person greeting line Elvi — Dressed to impress and make a multiple singular impression. Contact: Baskow & Associates. **702-733-7818**

Hispanic Elvis — Perhaps taking a cue from (the non-Las Vegas) El Vez, an agency will substitute the curled lip "Muchos gracias, muchos gracias" for "Thank you, thank you very much." Contact: Baskow & Associates. **702-733-7818**

Teen Elvis — Justin Shandor is the hottest Elvis on the horizon. The first time I saw him was in 2002, when he won an all-comers Elvis contest at age 17, beating out one of the top Elvi on the Strip. "I got teased out of school," Shandor told me. "They teased me so much about looking like Elvis, I said 'Why not try it?' " He often performs at the Elvis-O-Rama museum, 3401 Industrial Road. But as soon as he turns 21, he's going places.

Elvis morning meeting openers — Dress your CEO or VIP's in Elvis costumes. Have Elvis roar into your convention room on a Harley. No wonder people like to have their corporate meetings here. Contact: Baskow & Associates, **702-733-7818**; or Always Entertaining, **702-737-3232**.

Kelvis — With tongue planted firmly in cheek, Kelly Clinton bills herself as Kelvis, love child of Elvis and Ann-Margret. A former backup singer for Wayne Newton and Engelbert Humperdinck, Clinton is a fixture of the All-Elvis Choir. She's also the karaoke headliner at the Bootlegger on Mondays, usually sharing the mic with the likes of Clint Holmes, Sheena Easton, Lance Burton and friends. **702-838-4684**

Gay/Drag Queen Elvis — Gay Elvis is notice-ably light in the loafers and makes a grand entrance in a flaming red jumpsuit. As for Drag Queen Elvis, that whirring sound is The King spinning his grave. Contact: Baskow & Associates. **702-733-7818**.

Little People Elvis — "He's adorable," said Kelvis. "He also does a very funny Sonny and Cher with a huge Cher." Contact: Baskow & Associates. **702-733-7818**

Twin Elvi — The King was a twin (you did know that, right?) Now imagine if there had been two Kings. Contact: Baskow & Associates. **702-733-7818**

🌶 CRAZIEST MOMENTS FOR THE CRAZY GIRLS

Producer Norbert Aleman opened *Crazy Girls*, an American version of the Crazy Horse Saloon, in September 1987 at the Riviera. It has endured to be one of the longest running shows on the Strip, and there have been about 150 Crazy Girls. The emcees have included Jahna Steele, Pudgy, Bambi Jr. (Montel Williams' ex-wife), Carole Montgomery and most recently, the first male cast member, Joe Trammel.

— "One night a wife got jealous and her husband just sat there, staring at the floor for the whole show." — Karen Raider.

— "A guy came in and sat in the front row with a stash of one dollar bills, like we were going to do lap dances." — Marla Gomes.

— Heidi Deering had her picture taken with a celebrity after a *Crazy Girls* show. "We went out a couple times and he called me on my birthday. We had the same birthday." It was actor Joe Pesci, who was in Las Vegas filming *Casino*.

— "When Jim Carrey was filming (the Andy Kaufman biography) *Man in the Moon*, he came in and sat in the crowd dressed in character as Tony Clifton. He didn't crack a smile during the whole show." — Karen Raider.

— "When I was in *Enter the Night* (at the Stardust), one of the topless dancers fell off the stage and onto a table. All of the showgirls paraded by without offering to help her." — Kelly Adkins (who appeared in the *Ocean's Eleven* remake in a strip club scene with Brad Pitt).

— "One of the girls, as she was going sideways, ran right into a pole." — Tammie Rankin.

—"A guy fell asleep right in the front row. I tapped him twice with my foot and he woke up clapping like he was awake the whole time." — Rayna Alfred.

— "I was doing a show in Japan and my top broke. I had to do the whole show topless. And it wasn't a topless show." — Eve Letourneau.

— "Seeing my father in the front row, the first time he saw the show. And I was topless." – Heidi Deering, 18 at the time.

— "This guy showed up every day for a month to watch me in the show. He would play solitaire on the table anytime I wasn't on stage. He sent me a weird video tape of himself backstage.

The girls had to lie and tell him I was married so he finally went away." — Kelly Adkins, who appeared in *Ocean's Eleven*.

WILD THINGS (Rides & Attractions)

AJ Hackett Bungy — If you find the rides inside Circus Circus too tame, step outside and try a 171-foot plunge toward a 13-foot deep, 95,000-gallon pool. Water touches are available on Thursdays (locals day), Saturdays and Sundays. 810 Circus Circus Drive. **702-385-4321**

Big Shot — *Forbes FYI* magazine once named the Stratosphere Tower's pinnacle thrill ride the country's "best adrenalin rush." Tom Cruise and Nicole Kidman gave it a shot before splitting. It soars 160 vertical feet in seconds. Wimps to the rear. Stratosphere. **702-380-7777**

The Canyon Blaster — Two loops and two corkscrews highlight this 90-second thriller of a roller coaster inside the Adventuredome. Circus Circus. **702-794-3912**

CART Driving 101 — If simulators don't do it for you anymore, try a real race car experience at the Las Vegas Motor Speedway. Ride or drive in a two-seat Indy car at speeds up to 165 mph on the same track where the big boys race. Must be at least 18 and have a driver's license. 6001 Las Vegas Blvd. North, **702-644-4444** or **(877) 227-8101**; **www.driving101.com**.

Flyaway Indoor Skydiving — Experience simulated skydiving at 115 mph in a wind tunnel. Pop singer Jewel and her bronc-busting boyfriend

Ty Murray loved it. 200 Convention Center Drive. **702-731-4768**

Inverter — This one ranks among the highest in positive feedback. After plunging forward, riders are hurled backward and flipped 360 degrees. Circus Circus. **702-794-3939**

X Scream — The Stratosphere went over the edge when it added the *X Scream* extreme thrill ride in late 2003. Eight passengers experience free-fall at 30 mph on a tracked vehicle that slides 29 feet over the edge of the Stratosphere at 900 feet. Stratosphere. **702-380-7777**

Manhattan Express Roller Coaster — Experience some of the steepest drops in roller coasterdom and the sensation of a full barrel roll right above traffic on the Strip. Celebs who have tried it: Mariah Carey, Rob Lowe, Kelly Osbourne and Ann-Margaret, who lost her scarf. New York-New York. **702-740-6969**

Speed: The Ride — This $6-million ride rockets out the front of NASCAR Cafe, does a 79-foot loop at 70 mph, then shoots straight up a steel-tracked pole to 224 feet before making the return trip in reverse. If Granny goes along, you might want to tuck her false teeth in a safe place. Sahara. **702-737-2111**

High Roller — If you have issues with heights you better stick to the wading pool at Wet 'n Wild. This roller coaster sits at about 1,000 feet, circling the top deck of the Stratosphere Tower. Stratosphere. **702-380-7777**

AFTERTHOUGHTS AND STRAY NOTES FROM THE ROY HORN TIGER BITE STORY

It was a strange, startling end to a larger-than-life career: Roy Horn, the animal-training half of Siegfried & Roy, bitten in the neck by one of his beloved white tigers, onstage, on his 59th birthday — October 3, 2003. The national press descended on Las Vegas on this rare occasion where real-life drama collided with a show-business image that had been carefully sculpted over the years.

What was behind the public relations campaign to portray the white tiger Montecore as trying to "protect" Roy? Most likely it was a case of protecting the assets. After all, The Secret Garden of Siegfried & Roy attraction generates more than $7 million a year in admissions from 750,000 visitors annually, and millions more in merchandising. The *Father of the Pride* sitcom, airing fall 2004 on NBC, will be worth millions more.

In retrospect, the real miracle and testimony to Horn's training skills may be the fact that no serious incidents occurred during the 20,000-plus shows that came before that final night.

Several months before the mauling, Siegfried & Roy dancer Meagen Hensley of Anaconda, Montana, related what she termed a "spooky" incident. One of Horn's younger white tigers had to be restrained from going into a mock audience made up of cast members. She said the tiger "wanted to come out on the tables and say 'Hi.' " Hensley told *The (Butte) Montana Standard* that dancers routinely sat at tables in the theater during rehearsals to get the younger cats accustomed to performing before a crowd. "To me, that's scary," Hensley said. "That's 600 pounds of playful." All 63 big cats were in the show at one time.

Michael Jackson was among the few who were allowed to visit Horn in his University Medical Center hospital room. They have been friends for more than 20 years, from the mid-'70s era when Siegfried & Roy performed in the MGM Grand's *Hallelujah Hollywood* while the Jackson Five worked the same hotel's celebrity showroom. In fact, Jackson wrote and performed the theme song for *Siegfried & Roy at The Mirage*.

Among the jokes that had to be cut by local headliners after the mauling was this line by Monte Carlo magician Lance Burton, when ducks appear on stage and follow him: "A lot easier to train than white tigers."

Robert De Niro and Alec Baldwin playing Roy? When he hosted *Saturday Night Live* in December 2002, DeNiro, as Roy, complains to Donatella Versace, played by Maya Rudolph, that Roy is unhappy Siegfried isn't spending the holiday with him. At the end of the show, Roy is reunited with Siegfried, played by special guest Harvey Keitel. *SNL* again turned its sights on the duo for a post-bite sketch in November 2003, with Alec Baldwin as Roy being attacked by a turtle after the tiger prove too dangerous.

What was the approximate worth of Siegfried and Roy? Spies tell me Siegfried told friends he had about $75 million in the bank before Horn was injured.

Roy became a popular Halloween costume just four weeks after his accident. ABC late-night host Jimmy Kimmel told this story on his show a couple days after Halloween: A movie executive dressed as Siegfried, with an attacking stuffed animal on his shoulder, walked into a Los Angeles hotel on his way to a Halloween party. As the executive entered the hotel, he ran into the real Siegfried, who wasn't too happy about the getup. Kimmel said the story could have been an urban legend, but the hotel was across the street from the hospital where Horn was under treatment. I asked Bernie Yuman, Siegfried & Roy's manager, if he could confirm it. "I think I would have heard about it if that happened," he said.

One of the most bizarre aftershocks occurred when the 2004 Siegfried & Roy calendar came out six weeks after the mauling. Featured in the centerfold was none other than Montecore himself. By sheer coincidence, Horn had selected the tiger many months earlier. "We rotate the cats, whether it is for the marquee, the billboards or calendars. It was Roy's choosing who he would like to be up front and center," said Yuman, adding that the calendar was already in print and "put to bed six to eight months" earlier.

Just as eerie: In my newspaper column, I reported this sighting on October 23, 2002: "Sonya Fitzpatrick, the 'Pet Psychic' on Animal Planet, touring Siegfried & Roy's Secret Garden and Dolphin Habitat on Monday with Robert Wagner and Jill St. John. Fitzpatrick, of course, spent time conversing with the big cats." Which begs the question: What did they tell her?

Local producer Dick Feeney was at ground zero for the launch of the airborne Elvis phenomenon. Shortly after *Honeymoon in Vegas* started filming here in 1991, the call went out for some stunt men who would dress up as Elvis and make a parachute jump for the movie's finale. Feeney just happened to have an extensive wardrobe of Elvis jumpsuits and a lengthy contact list. When the movie opened in 1992 and the calls started flooding in for the squad of Elvis paratroopers, Feeney put together an aerial team and they've been flying high ever since. They have jumped onto cruise ships off the coast of Florida and delivered pizzas at San Diego Padres games. "A software company wanted us to jump as penguins for the Comdex convention. Super Dave wanted to hire us to do a jump as The Flying Ray Charles Brothers," said Feeney, who couldn't see it. Feeney nixed a proposal from Mars Candy. "It's the best request we never did. They were going to launch a new candy bar and wanted the Flying Elvi to toss them down to 10,000 people. Do you know what a candy bar would feel like at 200 mph? It's a bullet. "During one of the many events, Feeney told the crowd over the PA system that "the Elvi have left the building" and the newly coined name stuck.

Chapter 6
Entertainment: Classic Vegas

In Las Vegas, the past is as bright as the boldest neon. Some acts were diamonds, some turned to dust. For some starry-eyed dancers, Sin City was a stepping stone to bigger and better things. But for every career that soared here, others crashed like cheap cymbals. We toast the risk-takers who made it happen.

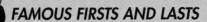
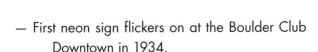
— First neon sign flickers on at the Boulder Club Downtown in 1934.

— First topless show (with no pasties) was *Minsky's Follies*, at the Dunes, January 10, 1957.

— Elvis' first Las Vegas date was April 23, 1956 at the New Frontier.

— Elvis' last (of 837) Las Vegas shows at the Hilton was December 12, 1976. (which is also Frank Sinatra's birthday).

— Frank Sinatra's first Las Vegas booking was September 4, 1951, Desert Inn.

— Sinatra's last Las Vegas show was May 29, 1994, MGM Grand Hotel.

— Dean Martin's first Las Vegas booking was March 6, 1957, when a curious crowd showed up at the Sands to see if Dino still had an act without Jerry Lewis.

— The Rat Pack's *Summit at the Sands* was January 20, 1960, concurrent with *Ocean's Eleven* location filming through February 16. The last time Sinatra, Dean Martin and Sammy Davis Jr. stood on a Las Vegas stage together was October 29, 1987, when Martin and Davis "surprised" The Chairman of the Board on his opening night at Bally's, where the other two already performed separately.

— Liberace's first Las Vegas show was November 24, 1944, at the Last Frontier, his home for the next eight years. Liberace's last Las Vegas show was August 11, 1986, at Caesars Palace. (He died February 4, 1987.)

— Sammy Davis Jr.'s first local appearance was in 1945, when he took the stage at the El Rancho Inn with his father and uncle in the Will Mastin Trio. His last show was at Harrah's in Lake Tahoe in 1989. The last time the public saw Davis perform was on February 4, 1990 during a taped TV tribute show in his honor. He took the stage and did a brief soft-shoe number.

 TOP 10 HEADLINER FLOPS

This list comes from Don Usherson, longtime entertainment reporter and columnist, who has witnessed more failure on the Strip than most of us could stand.

Mary Hart — The leggy co-host of *Entertainment Tonight* opened a 1988 David Brenner stint at the Golden Nugget with an act that was more Iowa summer stock than Vegas nightclub. Curious critics were quick to spread the bad news with pithy headlines such as "E.T. go home!" Hart never performed in Las Vegas again.

Ted Knight — The star of TV's *The Mary Tyler Moore Show* and *Too Close For Comfort* flopped so badly in the early '80s with a comedy and ventriloquist routine that he begged guests in his dressing room to put him out of his misery. "I don't belong here," he lamented of the gig as Jim Nabors' MGM Grand opening act. "I'm not a stand-up comic. I'm a TV star." Hotel Boss Bernie Rothkopf agreed and immediately fired him. Susan Anton replaced him the next night. Apparently, the live audience also was "too close for comfort."

Mario Lanza — The huge opera star (literally and figuratively) was scheduled to make his Las Vegas debut by opening the remodeled New Frontier in 1956. He was a no-show on the first of his scheduled 14 nights, choosing instead to party at the Sands with that hotel's boss Jack Entratter, columnist Louella Parsons and others. Several other Strip stars, including opening comedian Larry Storch, Jimmy Durante and Ray Bolger, covered for him that night. Lanza left Vegas the next day and never returned.

Denny McLain — The major league baseball pitching star had just won 31 games in 1968 when he decided to take to the Riviera stage, singing and playing his portable Hammond organ just a few weeks after his Detroit Tigers won the World Series. The hotel couldn't find a relief pitcher fast enough.

Elvis Presley — He had a disastrous debut at the New Frontier in 1956. The adult-oriented audiences of mid-'50s Vegas weren't ready for the still-juvenile strains of rock 'n' roll.

Ronald Reagan — In 1954, the head of the Screen Actors Guild and future California governor headlined the Last Frontier. Voters of the 1980s found him more convincing when he ran for president.

Djan Tatlian — After Communists in the Soviet Union turned away from his talent, he turned away from them and came to Las Vegas' own Imperial Palace in the early '80s. Audiences agreed with the Soviets and said, "Nyet."

Jim Varney — After huge success as lovable hick Ernest P. Worrell of TV commercial (and later movie) fame, Varney took his "Hey Vern" bit to the old Maxim in the mid-'80s. Audiences didn't get the humor any more than Vern did.

Silvi Vartan — Who? Exactly. She spent tons of money in the late '70s to promote herself as a huge international star, attempting to explode on the Vegas scene at the MGM Grand. Her explosion was, in fact, a bomb.

Walter Winchell — The famed New York gossip columnist attempted to re-create his radio show on the stage of the Tropicana in 1958. He saved face by donating what little proceeds there were from his two-week gig to charity.

 ## TOP 10 PRODUCTION SHOW FLOPS

Don Usherson again, reminding us that while it may be lonelier to fail by yourself, you can also take the entire Notre Dame cathedral down with you.

Alcazar — Desert Inn mogul Burton Cohen imported this revue after making several trips to Europe in the early '80s. To this day, no one can translate what it was all about.

Elvis: An American Musical — The Las Vegas Hilton tried to cash in on its ties to the Elvis myth by hosting this pretentious *Beatlemania*-style tribute in 1988. Audiences couldn't wait for all three of its Elvis-impersonator stars to leave the building.

The House of Love — Jayne Mansfield's third attempt to become a Las Vegas star crashed at the Dunes in 1960. The show may have flopped because her husband, former Mr. Universe Mickey Hargitay, showed much more skin onstage than she did.

Ipi Tombi — This international show was supposedly transplanted from a jungle somewhere when it played the Aladdin in the early '80s. The only thing memorable was the name, which, for a decade or so, became synonymous with all bad shows.

Men Are From Mars, Women Are From Venus — The familiarity of John Gray's self-help book should have made this original musical a big hit when it opened at the Flamingo in 2001. Instead, audiences decided the show was from Uranus.

Nebulae — More money was spent on promoting this nebulous Russian import at the Venetian in 2001 than the disco-singing Russians ever took in at the box office. Rehearsals lasted longer than the actual engagement.

Notre Dame de Paris — Based on the Victor Hugo classic better-known to Americans as *Hunchback of Notre Dame*, this original musical at Paris Las Vegas in 2000 was pronounced the most depressing show ever staged in Las Vegas. If Quasimodo had to sit in the audience for this maudlin pop opera, he would've killed himself and Esmerelda.

Opryland Country — The only thing memorable about this Nashville-based flop at the Boomtown (now Silverton) was Patsy Cline's hit "Crazy." Hotel management was even thinking of using it for their TV commercials after the show was canned… "Crazy, crazy for booking this show."

Rent — Granted, it was a Broadway hit. But it was a bad fit for the Las Vegas Hilton in 1999. The touring production never overcame technical problems or a painfully long script. Hotel personnel verified many patrons left at intermission thinking the show was over and not realizing they were breaking their leases.

Top Secret — Critics said this Sands effort of the early '80s should have remained a secret.

FROM VEGAS TO BIGGER AND BETTER THINGS

Barbara Jane Blakeley — This former Riviera showgirl first caught the eye of Zeppo Marx, straight man of the Marx Brothers. After their 10-year marriage ended, she married Frank Sinatra on July 11, 1976. In real estate, that's known as trading up.

Drew Carey — The sitcom star once was a Las Vegas bank clerk in the 1970s, honing his raw comedic skills by night at the Mine Shaft, a since-closed restaurant in the Commercial Center on East Sahara Avenue. He lived at the Blue Angel, a seedy motel on Fremont Street.

Violet Francis Irvin — She first came to Las Vegas in the 1950s and was hired as a chorus line dancer and singer at the Silver Slipper. She changed her name to Georgia Lee and, after moving to Florida, met and married NFL owner Carroll Rosenbloom. She was 30; he was 52.

After Rosenbloom drowned, his wife went on to become the first female owner of a Super Bowl-winning team, the St. Louis Rams.

Jimmy Kimmel — Here's a star who actually grew up in Las Vegas, after his family moved from Brooklyn when he was 9. An obsession with David Letterman laid the foundation of his career. In high school, he got a job at college station KUNV-FM, thanks to program director Ken Jordan, who went on to become half of electronica act *The Crystal Method*.

Bobbie Gentry — She was a *Les Folies Bergere* showgirl at age 17, but country music was her calling. In 1967, her crossover smash hit "Ode to Billy Joe" was No. 1 for four weeks. When she came back to Las Vegas in 1968, it was to headline at Caesars Palace.

Teri Garr — She was only 13 when she appeared in *Viva Las Vegas* as a showgirl. "It was my first job, and after that I did six movies with Elvis," she told me by phone in 2002. "I was working with a choreographer (in Los Angeles), David Winters, and Ann-Margret was in our dance class. She requested that David be the choreographer for the show," Garr recalled. Six years later, Elvis remembered his dancers in July 1969 when he launched his comeback at The International, now the Las Vegas Hilton. "He brought us up for his opening," Garr said.

Goldie Hawn — This Desert Inn chorus girl of the 1960s ended up winning the 1969 Academy Award for Best Supporting Actress for her first featured film role, in *Cactus Flower*.

Valerie Perrine — She was a lisping 18-year-old college student when her dad went broke in Scottsdale, Arizona. Having only ballet and tap dancing to fall back on, she decided to find a job in Las Vegas, where she spent six years at the Desert Inn and two at the Stardust, a nude lead in the latter. Still with no acting background, she eventually moved to Hollywood and landed the role of Montana Wildhack in the movie version of Kurt Vonnegut's Slaughterhouse Five. "I was smoking dope and just thought it was a giggle. I kind of expected it all. I'm weird. I take what life gives me," she told me during the Stardust's 45th anniversary on July 8, 2003. Two years later, she got her breakout role as Lenny Bruce's stripper wife in Lenny, with Dustin Hoffman. She was nominated for Best Actress, but her career sort of went up in smoke.

Joe Pesci — The scary movie mobster as a Vegas lounge act? It happened. "Joe would play guitar while I drummed, and we would exchange jokes," recalls Frank Vincent, who had a smaller role in *Casino* as Frank Marino. Pesci still loves Las Vegas and has talked with Mayor Oscar Goodman about partnering up as owners of a downtown speakeasy.

Kenny Rogers — Lounge-goers of the '60s might have seen him as part of the Bobby Doyle Three in the Thunderbird lounge. He was back in the lounges in 1977 after a brush with fame in the First Edition. "I had dinner with him about that time and he was at wit's end," recalled Bill Medley of the Righteous Brothers. "He said, 'I'm doing some country stuff in Nashville,' and country music of course wasn't what it is today. Then he exploded."

— The highly promoted NBC series Las Vegas brought the Strip back to prime time in the fall of 2003. But it would have to stay on the air a long time to push out my fond '70s memories of VEGA$ and a certain T-bird cruising the Strip. The light-hearted action drama from TV trash-meister Aaron Spelling aired on ABC from 1978 to 1981.

— Robert Urich played Las Vegas private eye Dan Tanna, who drives a flashy 1957 T-Bird. In the show, his office is in the Desert Inn, which is owned by Philip Roth (Tony Curtis). But the set was actually at 2780 Las Vegas Blvd. South, which became the Guinness World Of Records Museum in 1990. "We still get mail addressed to Dan Tanna delivered to the museum," said Oli Lewis, general manager of the museum.

— Dan Tanna meets Charlie's Angels? It happened February 9, 1977, during the first season of Charlie's Angels. ABC, in a crossover, had the Angels — Kate Jackson, Farrah Fawcett, Jaclyn Smith — go to Las Vegas on a case, where they just happened to "run" into Dan Tanna.

— Phyllis Davis, who played Beatrice Travis, Tanna's super-hot and savvy secretary, became romantically involved with Dean Martin during the series. I sat across from her at the Desert Inn's 50th anniversary in April 2000, and believe me, she was still turning heads. She mentioned she had spent a number of years living in the Bay area and was into a holistic lifestyle. She volunteered that her relationship with Dino was a difficult one.

— Dominic Frontiere, who wrote the theme to *VEGA$*, later married Georgia Rosenbloom, owner of the Los Angeles Rams and Super Bowl-winning St. Louis Rams.

— Tanna's warehouse "home" featured a garage door that allowed him to drive his 1957 red T-Bird convertible car right into the middle of his house. Once he drove in, he would always hop out over the car door and be standing in the middle of his living room.

— The former movie-set home of Dan Tanna is on display at the Guinness World of Records on the Strip.

— Stepfanie Kramer made one appearance, in 1980 at age 24, before finding fame in *Hunter* from 1984 to 1990 as Detective Sergeant Dee Dee McCall, partner of Detective Sergeant Rick Hunter (Fred Dryer).

— Urich died of cancer on April 16, 2002. The trivia book *10,000 Answers: The Ultimate Trivia Encyclopedia*(Random House Reference, 2001) claimed Urich the record for starring in the most TV shows: 15.

— Because so much of the series was shot on location in Las Vegas, casting heavily involved headliners who were performing on the Strip. Mamie Van Doren appeared as a spa manager, Sid Caesar as a general, Red Buttons as minister, Morey Amsterdam as a lion owner, George Jessel as a eulogist, band leader Doc Severinsen as himself and Elvis squeeze Linda Thompson and an up-and-coming Kim Basinger (only 24 and three years away from getting a big-screen part) as eye candy.

 ## *TOP 10 LAS VEGAS MOVIES*

Bugsy (1991) — New York gangster Ben "Bugsy" Siegel (Warren Beatty) gets the big idea that the mob ought to turn Las Vegas into a '40s playground for the rich and famous. But he gets greedy. The top-shelf cast includes Annette Bening, Harvey Keitel, Ben Kingsley, Elliott Gould, Joe Mantegna and Bebe Neuwirth. The Flamingo reproduction had to be built in California because there wasn't enough left of the original here.

Casino (1995) — The ultimate Las Vegas mob movie. Robert De Niro and Joe Pesci play mobbed-up pals who end up fighting each other, the feds and a money-mad woman (Sharon Stone) in the '70s, when organized crime is losing its grip on Las Vegas. Mob attorney Oscar Goodman has a cameo (four years later he was overwhelmingly voted in as Las Vegas mayor). One novelty is the casting of comedians Alan King, Dick Smothers, Kevin Pollak and Don Rickles in dramatic roles.

Con Air (1997) — Nicolas Cage as Cameron Poe, a decorated U.S. Ranger, is finally getting out of jail after serving an eight-year term for manslaughter. The wife he protected during a fatal bar fight waits with their daughter. But convicts take over the transport plane and plan to escape to a foreign country. They end up heading for Las Vegas. The supporting rogues gallery includes Steve Buscemi, David Chappelle, John Malkovich and Ving Rhames.

Diamonds Are Forever (1971) — It's not among the elite James Bond films, but a hoot nonetheless with all of the scenes of Vegas at the dawn of the corporate era. It was supposed to be Sean Connery's last turn as James Bond, and this one didn't do him any favors. Still he returned 13 years later in *Never Say Never Again.* Jill St. John is the Bond girl in this Vegas voyage, appropriately enough, given her past ties to Frank Sinatra. Charles Gray is the villain who kidnaps Jimmy Dean, playing the casino tycoon who is Howard Hughes by everything but the name.

Honeymoon in Vegas (1992) — What a plot: Nicolas Cage's commitment-phobic character heads to Las Vegas with girlfriend (Sarah Jessica Parker) and they decide to get married. James Caan enters the picture as a big-time gambler who has eyes for Parker and arranges for Cage to lose $65,000 at poker. Caan's character offers to take care of the debt in exchange for a weekend with the girlfriend. Boyfriend has a last-minute moment of clarity, flies into a jealous rage and ends up rescuing his damsel by hitching a ride on a plane full of flying Elvis impersonators.

Leaving Las Vegas (1995) — Cage going for the Las Vegas trifecta, but this one with a dark shift in tone from the other two. This time he is Ben Sanderson, a just-fired alcoholic who decides to end it all in Las Vegas with a month of binge drinking. He falls in love with Sera (Elisabeth Shue), a prostitute who tells him, "That's nice talk, Ben. Keep drinking. Between the 101-proof breath and the occasional bits of drool, some interesting words come out."

Ocean's Eleven (1960) — Frank Sinatra and his Rat Pack pals team up as 11 World War II vets with a grand plan to knock off five Las Vegas casinos on the same night. But even the best-laid plans … Dean Martin, Sammy Davis Jr., Joey Bishop and Peter Lawford famously joined Sinatra on stage every night while the production was filming in town.

Ocean's Eleven (2001) — New Las Vegas never shines brighter than in this star-studded remake which realizes the comic suspense possibilities mostly ignored in the Rat Pack version. This time around, George Clooney is heistmeister Danny Ocean and his team of professionals target three casinos on the night of a major heavyweight fight. Fresh angle: The hotels are operated by tough-nutted Terry Benedict (Andy Garcia), whose love interest is Ocean's ex-wife Tess (Julia Roberts). Director Steven Soderbergh delivers lots of laughs and high-tech equipment. The all-star team includes Matt Damon, Brad Pitt, Don Cheadle, Bernie Mac, Elliott Gould and Carl Reiner.

Rain Man (1988) — Money-grubbing Charlie Babbitt (Tom Cruise) finds out that his dead father has left a fortune to an autistic brother (Dustin Hoffman) who has been institutionalized. Charlie kidnaps his brother to get the money and they head for California in an antique convertible. Along the way, Charlie finds out his brother has an incredible talent for figuring out mathematical problems at warp speed; a skill that gives Charlie big plans in Las Vegas.

Viva Las Vegas (1964) — The fifteenth of more than 30 films Elvis made between 1956 and

1972, this one is best remembered for the King's off-camera romance with Ann-Margret and for the title song, still going strong as the city's anthem. Director George Sidney, the king of movie musicals at the time, came up with the title and made the most of the duo's sizzling chemistry. Elvis plays a race car driver in town to compete in the Las Vegas Grand Prix; Ann-Margret's character manages the Flamingo swimming pool. He loses the cash for a new engine and must work as a waiter. They hit it off, and sing and dance all the way to the finish line.

 MEMORABLE VEGAS MOVIE SCENES

Bugsy (1991) — The final panoramic shot of the Strip in the 1990s, reminding us of what Bugsy's vision in the desert had blossomed into.

Casino (1995) — That slow-motion scene when "Ace" Rothstein (Robert De Niro) first sets eyes on his future wife Ginger (Sharon Stone), winning big and throwing chips after a big score at the gaming tables. Trying to mate with a Komodo dragon would have been a better move.

Con Air (1997) — The crash of the prison transport plane into the Sands Hotel, after clipping the guitar sign off the front of the Hard Rock Hotel.

The Electric Horseman (1979) — Robert Redford riding the white stallion through the casino at Caesars Palace. "Stallions are known to be high-strung so we spent months training him," director Sydney Pollack told me. "We played a tape recording of slot machine sounds for hours in his stall. He behaved better than the actors."

Honeymoon in Vegas (1992) —The Elvis impersonators parachuting into the Bally's parking lot. Duh.

Ocean's Eleven (2001) — The parting scene in front of the Bellagio's dancing fountains, as the gang members contemplate their good fortunes to the strains of "Claire de Lune."

Lost in America (1985) — David Howard (Albert Brooks) discovering that his wife Linda (Julie Hagerty) had sneaked down to the casino and lost their life savings in an overnight gambling binge at the Desert Inn.

Ocean's Eleven (1960) — The Rat Pack, walking away from the Sands in the final scene, with their real names coming into view behind them on the hotel marquee.

Rain Man (1988) — That moment when Charlie (Tom Cruise) and Raymond (Dustin Hoffman) appear on the escalator at Caesars Palace in matching suits, going for the big score on the strength of Raymond's card-counting ability.

Viva Las Vegas (1964) — Elvis singing "Viva Las Vegas" for the first time, in the talent contest scene.

Mike Weatherford, *Review-Journal* entertainment reporter, delved into the campier side of Las Vegas moviemaking for his book, *Cult Vegas — The Weirdest! The Wildest! The Swingin'est Town on Earth!*

The Atomic Kid (1954) — Slapstick fun with an irradiated Mickey Rooney at the Nevada Test Site.

Destiny Turns on the Radio (1995) — This one was made during the Quentin Tarantino craze (he acts in it) and tried too hard to be a cult movie. You can't try to be a cult movie. Ask the makers of *3,000 Miles to Graceland*.

The Grasshopper (1969) — A "Summer of Love" melodrama starring a shagadelic Jacqueline Bisset that can't decide if it's groovin' with the hippies or down with The Man.

Indecent Proposal (1992) — Woody Harrelson goes from cute *Cheers* bartender to natural born killer after freaking out over talking robots and Shriners in the Las Vegas Hilton's Benihana restaurant.

Las Vegas Hillbillys (1966)— It had to be included because of the title. But what a cheat that only one scene — a jalopy sputtering along the Strip — was really filmed in Las Vegas.

Las Vegas Lady (1976) — Stella Stevens woos Stuart Whitman as both compete to see who can sport the tackiest '70s hair, while people climb around the outside of Circus Circus in this low-rent variation on the *Ocean's Eleven* heist plot.

Las Vegas Weekend (1985) — A nerd takes his mathematical "system" to Glitter Gulch. People stare as he walks down Fremont Street. Like no one's ever seen a nerd on Fremont Street.

Lookin' to Get Out (1982) — A good movie at times threatens to get out of this bizarre buddy picture in which Burt Young does a lot of shouting at Jon Voight. The opening credits offer rare footage of Siegfried & Roy in the MGM Grand's *Hallelujah Hollywood!* revue.

Showgirls (1995) — The team behind *Basic Instinct* delivers drive-in trash that rings false in almost every aspect. It's almost too seedy to play as camp, if not for Gina Gershon's *Valley of the Dolls*-worthy performance.

3,000 Miles to Graceland (2001) — Like *Showgirls*, it has an arch humor to its crudeness and could have been fun slumming if it wasn't so self-aware or knew when to quit. A movie about Elvis impersonators robbing a casino — guarded by a machine-gun toting Paul Anka! — that's not an out-an-out comedy? *Hello-o-o-o.*

 ## TOP 10 RAT PACK LINES

"And now, direct from the bar..." — Joey Bishop, introducing Dean Martin.

"I'd like to thank the NAACP for this trophy." — Martin, picking up Sammy Davis Jr. and cradling him in his arms. Witnesses say Joey Bishop had just whispered the line in Martin's ear, but it became a faithful part of any Rat Pack show.

"We feel sorry for people who don't drink because when they wake up in the morning, that's as good as they're gonna feel all day!" — Martin, appropriating the line originated by Joe E. Lewis.

"I'm for whatever gets you through the night, be it prayer, tranquilizers or a bottle of Jack Daniels!" — Frank Sinatra.

"I drink to make other people interesting." — Martin.

"This is my first drink all day... with my left hand!" — Martin.

"Ring a ding-ding, baby!" — Sinatra.

"It's post time!" — Sinatra, lifting another Joe E. Lewis line when raising a drink.

"Here's to the confusion of our enemies!" — a Sinatra toast.

"Here's to absent friends. F--- 'em." — another Sinatra toast.

10 CLASSIC LIBERACE QUOTES

"I'm not good, but I've got guts!"

"Why don't I slip out and get into something more spectacular!"

"Too much of a good thing is wonderful."

"Remember that bank I cried all the way to? I bought it!"

"Mary Poppins, eat your heart out!"

"This costume is made out of virgin fox. It took forever to get the pelts. Think about it!"

"I've had so much fun tonight that, honestly, I'm ashamed to take the money. But I will."

"It's twenty rubies past nine diamonds."

"There's only two in the whole world like it, and I've got both of them!"

"People ask me how I tell time. I say, "Who cares, ask a friend.""

VEGAS OSCAR MOMENTS

No one ever expected *Viva Las Vegas* to win an Academy Award. But a few Las Vegas-related movies have walked away with Hollywood's top honors. The most easily remembered, for the title alone, is Nicolas Cage taking home the Best Actor award in 1995 for his role as the suicidal alcoholic in *Leaving Las Vegas*.

Right up there with it is *Rain Man*, which won Best Picture and three other Oscars in 1988: Dustin Hoffman, Best Actor; Barry Levinson, Best Director; and Ronald Bass and Barry Morrow for Original Screenplay.

Sharon Stone was at least in the running when she was nominated for Best Actress for *Casino*.

Other Vegas-related movies have at least scored technical honors including *Bugsy* (Best Art Direction-Set Decoration to Dennis Gassner and Nancy Haigh, and Best Costume Design to Albert Wolsky) and *The Electric Horseman* for Best Sound in 1980 (Les Fresholtz, Michael Minkler, Al Overton Jr. and Arthur Piantadosi).

Important dates and salary figures in the history of Las Vegas entertainment:

1944 — Liberace is hired in Las Vegas for $750 a week and sees it doubled within a week.

1947 — Gangster Bugsy Siegel, owner of the new and financially-strapped Flamingo, offers Liberace $2,000 per week to jump ship. Liberace stays put. Siegel is soon killed mob-style on June 20, 1947, in Los Angeles.

1951 — A troubled Frank Sinatra makes his Las Vegas headliner debut on September 4, 1951, at Wilbur Clark's Desert Inn. Only a few days before had come news that Sinatra, after a fight with Ava Gardner, attempted to commit suicide in Lake Tahoe. He denied it, calling it a sleeping-pill miscalculation. The Desert Inn engagement was not a hot ticket. "I was there at the time," recalled Sinatra pal Sonny King. "You could sit in the back and have a cola and not see many in heads in front of you; it was empty."

1953 — Shortly after Sinatra wins an Oscar for *From Here to Eternity*, the Sands Hotel signs him to a deal that includes 2 percent of the property — he paid $54,000 for the two points — and a salary believed to be about $25,000 a week. He makes his Sands debut on October 7. Two months later, film icon and cabaret singer Marlene Dietrich debuts at the Sahara on December 15 for a reported $35,000 per week, making her the highest paid performer in nightclub history.

1955 — Liberace tops that when the new Riviera lures him away from the New Frontier by doubling his check to $50,000 a week. He opens the elegant Clover Room on April 20.

1959 — Wayne Newton, 17, and brother Jerry travel from Phoenix to play the Fremont Hotel lounge for $280 per week, with $80 going to the musicians union and half of the remainder sent home to their parents. "We did six shows a night, six nights a week. Two weeks turned into 46 weeks the first year," Newton recalled.

1963 — Barbra Streisand receives $50,000 for her Las Vegas debut at the Riviera on August 2. "Liberace came in to rehearsal and said, 'Oh girls, wait till you see this new young singer,'" recalled longtime showgirl Betty Bunch. "He said, 'She's a little eccentric; buys her clothes at thrift shops. But what a voice." When Babs showed up for rehearsal, "We sat there in that dark showroom and when the Jack Cathcart Orchestra started playing her music, we all fell over when she opened her mouth. We were all stunned."

1967 — Siegfried & Roy sign on for a $700 per-week slot in the Tropicana's *Les Folies Bergere*. The hotel president tells them, "Magic don't work in this town."

1968 — "Mama" Cass Elliot, formerly of the Mamas and the Papas, gets $40,000 a week to play Caesars Palace but takes ill on opening night. Flip Wilson moves up from the second-billed spot to finish the run.

1969 — Elvis returns. The new International (which will become the Las Vegas Hilton) pays him

$125,000 a week, according to former road manager Joe Esposito. Four weeks later his salary is revised and a long-term deal struck. By the time of his August 1977 death, Elvis notches 867 sellouts at the hotel.

1972 — Liberace opens at the Las Vegas Hilton for $300,000 a week, the start of a 10-year commitment. By 1978, the *Guinness Book of World Records* will list him as the world's highest-paid musician, averaging $5 million per year for more than 35 years.

1978 — Siegfried and Roy become the headline act of the Stardust's *Lido de Paris* for $11,000-per-week the first year, $13,000 the second and $15,000 in the final year. As a bonus, the Stardust throws in a Silver Shadow Rolls Royce. In 1981, they get a $125,000 per-week deal at the Frontier.

1980 — Steve Wynn pays Frank Sinatra $10 million over three years to perform at Wynn's Golden Nugget properties in Las Vegas and Atlantic City.

1981 — Meshulam Riklis, owner of the Riviera, signs Dolly Parton to a new Las Vegas record of $350,000 for a one-week appearance. After opening night she claims to have "Vegas throat" from the dry air and cancels the rest of the week.

1982 — Cher pulls down $250,000 per week from Caesars Palace, but it doesn't seem so sweet when Francis Ford Coppola visits during the run and asks why her film career isn't happening. "I've tried, I've really tried," she tells the director. "Bullshit. You haven't tried hard enough," he replies. Las Vegas doesn't see her for the rest of the decade. In 1991, Steve Wynn pays her a reported $8 million to play multiple engagements at The Mirage.

1998 — Needing a big act to launch The Mirage, Wynn signs a $58.5 million deal with Siegfried and Roy for five years and a second five-year option. They made their debut at the Mirage on February 1, 1990.

1999 — Streisand rings in New Year's Eve at the MGM Grand Hotel. Fans pay as much as $2,500 for tickets. MGM later claims the concert is the highest-grossing of all-time, with gross revenues of $14,694,750, surpassing the previous record of $13.4 million set by the Three Tenors at Giants Stadium.

2000 — Impressionist Danny Gans moves from The Rio to The Mirage for a reported $25 million over eight years.

2001 — Celine Dion signs a three-year deal with Caesars Palace worth a reported $40-$50 million. Later, unconfirmed reports place the number as high as $100 million. Caesars builds a 4,000-seat Colosseum for her.

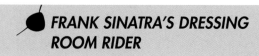

FRANK SINATRA'S DRESSING ROOM RIDER

These contractual requirements were included in Sinatra's 23-page technical rider for his New Year's Eve performances at The Riviera in 1990, 1991, and 1992.

— A map that indicated precisely where the upright piano was to be placed. Five bottles of liquor:

Absolut vodka, Jack Daniels, Chivas Regal, Courvoisier, Beefeater gin. Twelve rolls of cherry Lifesavers. One bag of miniature Tootsie Rolls. Twelve wine glasses. One carton of Camels (no filter). All sodas in all rooms should be 75 percent diet. Two bars of Ivory soap. Two chicken salad sandwiches (min. mayo). Local promoter is to provide on the evening of the show, an ear, nose & throat specialist with appropriate medication and sprays, including Decadron, to be at the arena from 5:30 p.m. to 11:00 p.m.

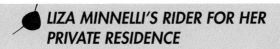

LIZA MINNELLI'S RIDER FOR HER PRIVATE RESIDENCE

Minnelli preferred a private residence to a hotel suite. Her November 1989 rider at The Riviera included 99 items, mostly food related. Here's a sampling:

— Fresh garlic (six heads). Six ripe tomatoes, two red peppers, two green peppers, two purple onions, 10 yellow onions and fresh mushrooms (one package). Five loaves of bread: sourdough, Italian, Oat (sliced), seeded rye bread (sliced), wheat (sliced) and Wonder/white (sliced). Jiffy Creamy Peanut Butter. I Can't Believe It's Not Butter. Oreo Cookies (two packages). Carton of Marlsboro cigarettes/fliptop box. Two ultra-sonic humidifiers, one in master bedroom and one in main sitting room. Fettucine, spaghetti, linguine,and white rice. Heavenly Hash ice cream.

On May 18, 1990, the day of the funeral of Sammy Davis Jr., the Strip went dark for 10 minutes in honor of arguably the greatest entertainer of them all. Davis' widow, Altovise, recalls caring for their three sons hours after the funeral in Los Angeles, when the TV newscast mentioned the lights-out Las Vegas tribute.

Unaware of the significance, one of the young boys turned to Altovise and asked, "Is that bad?"

"No,' I told him, 'It's a good thing.' "His epitaph at Forest Lawn Glendale reads: Sammy Davis Jr."The Entertainer" He Did It All.

Chapter 7

Back in the 'Bad' Old Days

From its start as a dusty train stop in 1905 to mobster Bugsy Siegel's vision of a desert paradise, the mythic rise of Las Vegas was always about someone taking a gamble. Here are some people and places that left an imprint in the sands of Old Las Vegas.

Courtesy of the late Frank Wright, curator of the Nevada State Museum & Historical Society.

June 14, 1855 — Mormons first camp along Las Vegas Creek and start building a fort.

May 15, 1905 — San Pedro Los Angeles and Salt Lake Railroad auction off lots in the new Las Vegas settlement.

March 19, 1931 — Gambling is legalized in Nevada.

1931 to 1936 — Construction of Hoover Dam leads to a growth spurt, doubling Southern Nevada's population from about 6,000 to almost 14,000. By 1950, it triples to 45,000 as Strip business soars.

April, 1941 — El Rancho Vegas becomes the first hotel on the Strip.

December 26, 1946 — Mobster Bugsy Siegel opens the Flamingo, planting the seeds for growth of the Las Vegas gambling industry.

January, 1960 — The Rat Pack brings an unprecedented showbiz buzz to the Strip.

Thanksgiving, 1966 — Howard Hughes arrives. "Las Vegas had gotten such a bad rap for mobsters and here was Hughes, with such a clean, heroic image," Wright said.

1969 — Corporate gaming law opens the way for publicly-traded corporations.

November, 1989 — Steve Wynn triggers the mega-resort era with completion of the Mirage. The ensuing growth is unprecedented, leading to 11 new resorts in 10 years: The Rio and Excaliber, 1990; Luxor, Treasure Island and MGM Grand, 1993; Monte Carlo, 1996; New York-New York, 1997; Bellagio, 1998; Venetian and Paris, 1999; and the new Aladdin, 2000.

 10 WILDEST WAGERS

— Benny Binion's Horseshoe was the epicenter of high-stakes action long before the World Series of Poker. Binion often boasted that he would take any bet. When William Lee Bergstrom let it be known he was interested in making a $1-million bet on a single roll of the dice, Binion put his money where his mouth is. In 1980, Bergstrom showed up carrying a suitcase stuffed with $770,000 and didn't bother to change it into chips. He put the suitcase on the "don't-pass" line and waited as a female patron prepared to toss the dice. She crapped out, making Bergstrom a winner. After getting paid, Bergstrom didn't stick around to celebrate. But he returned about a year later and tried it again, losing this time. A former FBI agent tells me Bergstrom died of suicide a few years later.

— Bob Martin, a bookmaker at Churchill Downs and the Union Plaza, lived for big bets. In 1980, a bettor reportedly went to Martin and put $1.5 million on the Rams, 11-point underdogs to the Pittsburgh Steelers in Super Bowl XIV. The Steelers won 31-19. Martin knew how to work the media. I know firsthand because I was an Associated Press reporter assigned to Las Vegas on a regular basis during the early 1980s. Martin was eminently available and quotable. When seismologists predicted Los Angeles was overdue for an earthquake, Martin put up 30-1 odds that the quake would not hit in July. He got his name out on the news wires again when scientists predicted a major meteor was on a collision course with Earth. Martin made Mexico the 8-1 favorite as the impact area.

— Retired NBA great Charles Barkley won $787,000 at Mandalay Bay when he bet $550,000 on the New England Patriots, plus the 14 points, in the 2002 Super Bowl against St. Louis, and then bet $50,000 on New England on the money line. Barkley won both bets when the Patriots stunned the Rams, 20-17. The bets cost sports book director Nick Bogdanovich his job, apparently because Barkley was given the betting slips without having a sufficient line of credit and did not sign a marker. Mandalay Bay had a casino host ask Barkley to cancel the bet but he declined and the casino paid up.

— Financier Carl Icahn bet $2.3 million at the Mirage to win $400,000 on the heavily favored San Francisco 49ers, wagering they would cover the 20-point spread against the San Diego Chargers in 1995s Super Bowl XXIX. San Francisco came through for him, 49-26.

— Bob Stupak, creator of The Stratosphere, won a $1 million Super Bowl bet in 1989 at Little Caesars, a tiny casino since leveled to make way for Paris Las Vegas. It was billed as the largest wager in Nevada history at the time. Stupak, the son of a Pittsburgh bookmaker, won when the Cincinnati Bengals lost to the San Francisco 49ers 26-21, but he covered the seven-point spread.

— Golfer Phil Mickelson, in a futures bet at the Bellagio sports book, put $20,000 on the Baltimore Ravens at 28-1 to win the 2001 Super Bowl — and hit a $560,000 jackpot. He probably won't be back, after I reported that he walked out without leaving a dime and ESPN grilled him about it. It's still not known whether it was a ballsy single bet or whether Mickelson laid down a few other futures bets at the same time.

— Amarillo Slim knew something was up when Steve Wynn approached him one day and asked if he knew how to play dominoes. Wynn informed him that Willie Nelson had won a national domino championship at age 19. He then proceeded to bet $50,000 and a Jeep Cherokee that Slim couldn't beat Nelson, who was so confident he bet $300,000 on himself, according to Slim's book, *Amarillo Slim in a World of Fat People*. But Amarillo Slim prevailed. "I was happy to take money from two men who had more than they needed," he wrote.

— Jimmy the Greek was a Las Vegas wise guy long before he made it to CBS as Brent Musberger's sidekick (and later slugged him in a barroom dustup). During the 1948 presidential election, bookmakers had Harry Truman a 60-to-1 underdog to Thomas Dewey, even though Truman was the incumbent. The Greek claims he surveyed 1,900 woman and found they didn't like men with a moustache. As the campaign went on, the odds came down to 17-to-1 and the Greek came up with $10,000 and put it on

Truman to win. Truman won and so did Jimmy the Greek, whose bet earned him $170,000 and a lot of juice in Nevada, where he set up the Vegas Turf and Sportsroom.

— Longtime Las Vegas bookmaker Sonny Reizner knew how to get his name out there too. I met him in the late 1980s and talked to him frequently while doing a gambling series for the *Rocky Mountain News*, about Bronco bettors who literally bet the house (one actually bet a couple months of mortgage money and lost his home) on the 1987 Super Bowl. Sonny's claim to fame came in 1980 when he put up odds on "Who Shot J.R.?" J.R. Ewing was a scheming oil tycoon on *Dallas*, the hit TV series. Sonny listed odds for everyone on the show, and even threw in Dallas Cowboys coach Tom Landry as a 500-1 long shot. But Nevada's Gaming Control Board made him take the bets off the board because the event didn't qualify as a sport and the outcome could be controlled from outside (the show had been taped months earlier).

— Steve Wynn is a businessman, not a gambler. But he won a $1 million bluff in 1971 and has been on a roll ever since. Wynn, who arrived in Las Vegas in 1967, saw a financial opportunity when he learned that a strip of land adjacent to Caesars Palace, on the corner of Las Vegas Boulevard and Flamingo Road, was not owned by Caesars. It was, in fact, the property of Howard Hughes, who wouldn't sell it to the owners of the Roman-themed hotel. "But nobody knew more about the Hughes real estate holdings than did Wynn's new mentor, Parry Thomas, who had helped assemble them," according to A.D. Hopkins, writing in *The First*

100: Portraits of the Men and Women Who Shaped Las Vegas. "Wynn located another land parcel that Hughes needed, obtained an option on it, and then arranged a swap with Hughes, snatching the Flamingo Road parcel from under Caesars' nose," Hopkins writes. Then Wynn announced plans to build the world's narrowest casino, forcing the hotel to buy the land for $2.25 million. Wynn and a partner split a profit of more than $1 million in the deal, according to the book, bankrolling Wynn's purchase of the Golden Nugget and the starting point of his casino empire.

 ## DUST-UPS IN THE DESERT

Sinatra vs. the Sands — On September 11, 1967, Frank Sinatra was punched in the mouth by Sands casino manager Carl Cohen, a gentle 250-pound man who reportedly said, "Frank who?" after leaving Sinatra with two broken caps on his front teeth. Sinatra was angry that Howard Hughes, the new owner, had passed down the word to cut off his credit. Sinatra went into a rage and drove a golf cart into a plate-glass window. The final straw came when he threw a chair toward Cohen, according to newspaper reports.

Hughes vs. the Mob — During the 1960s, Cleveland mobster-turned-hotelier Moe Dalitz ran the Desert Inn, which was part of the Las Vegas branch of Lucky Luciano's operation. When Howard Hughes moved to Las Vegas on Thanksgiving weekend of 1966, his headquarters became Penthouse One, a three-room suite on the ninth (top) floor of the Desert Inn. Dalitz reportedly was unimpressed that Hughes wasn't spending his millions in the casino and ordered him out, saying all the rooms were booked for New Year's. Hughes' response: He bought control of the hotel for $13.25 million, officially taking over on April 1, 1967.

Wayne Newton vs. Las Vegas newspaper columnist — In 1995, the acerbic *Review-Journal* entertainment critic Mike Paskevich described Newton's singing voice as "Kermit the Frog on steroids." After reading the review, Newton stormed into the newspaper and wanted Paskevich fired. When that didn't work, Newton later spotted Paskevich in the audience and stopped his show to lace into him. Paskevich subsequently wrote, "You can't keep a bad man down. After he closes his run in boring Branson, Missouri, in December, Wayne 'Midnight Idle' Newton and what's left of his voice will return home for a one-week engagement at the Desert Inn, January 16-21 (1996)."

Wayne Newton vs. Johnny Carson — These two had a long-running public feud, mainly over a tug-of-war to purchase the Aladdin Hotel. In January 1980, an agreement was reached for Johnny Carson, Ed Nigro and National Kinney Corp. to buy the Aladdin for $105 million. When the deal fell through, Newton jumped in and bought it for $85 million in a partnership with Valley Bank, the latter acting as trustee for the children of Edward Torres, former Riviera president. Carson proceeded to taunt Newton on his TV show, and one day the crooner decided he'd had enough. Newton tells it this way: "I walked into his office and said, 'This crap is gonna end or I'm gonna knock you on your ass!'" I was in town, on assignment with The Associated Press, and covered the Newton news conference where he announced a multi-million-dollar lawsuit against Carson. A few months later I received a call from Carson's attorney who said I might be called for a deposition. The call never came.

Michael Gaughan vs. MGM, Hilton, Caesars and Dunes — The Big Four wanted to turn a little corner of Las Vegas Boulevard at Flamingo Road into a parking lot, but Gaughan would have none of it. He held onto the property and turned it into the Barbary Coast. "Every day, somebody tries to buy it off me," Gaughan says of the prime piece of Strip real estate. "Arthur Goldberg (the late president and chief executive officer of Park Place Entertainment, who died in October, 2000) called all the time." But Gaughan's got too sweet of a deal to leave anytime soon. "I got 60 years to go on my lease and I pay $550 a day on the lease, about $200,000 a year. That's $550 a day on 1.7 acres. That land might be worth anywhere from $8 to 12 million."

Frank "Lefty" Rosenthal vs. Harry Reid — When the mob needed an inside man to keep tabs on their skimming operation at the Stardust in the 1970s, they turned to convicted sports fixer Rosenthal and his "muscle," Tony "The Ant" Spilotro. But Rosenthal was claiming he ran the place, and would need a state gaming license to continue his duties. The licensing issue reached critical mass in 1976, when Rosenthal's request was denied based on his criminal background. Reid, appointed to head the Nevada Gaming Commission in 1977, soon found himself under pressure from the *Las Vegas Sun* and *Valley Times*, who reversed their earlier stances favoring strict gambling regulation and began questioning the state gaming authority's power. There were suggestions that Rosenthal was a whipping boy. Rosenthal went to court with attorney Oscar Goodman, but lost the challenge in the Nevada Supreme Court. The end came for Rosenthal in December 1978, but the publicity-hound didn't go out with a whimper. When Reid and his colleagues voted unanimously to deny Rosenthal's application, Lefty made a scene at the hearing, taunting Reid in a heated public exchange.

Frank "Lefty" Rosenthal vs. the mob — Three years after the license was denied, Lefty was lucky to survive a car bombing on East Sahara Avenue. Fingers pointed toward Spilotro, who had become antagonistic toward Rosenthal as their relationship unraveled. "These guys were not very smart," a longtime Las Vegas gaming operator told me. "How do you miss a guy with a car bomb?" "It is said the bombing was Spilotro's downfall because the publicity angered the Chicago mob hierarchy. Spilotro was buried alive with his brother Michael in an Indiana cornfield in June 1986. Rosenthal eventually moved to Florida, no doubt for health reasons, and remains there. His name is still in Nevada's "black book" of excluded persons, banned for life from the state's casinos. Both men are immortalized in the 1995 film *Casino*, with Robert DeNiro cast as Rosenthal (renamed Ace Rothstein) and Joe Pesci as Nicky Santoro, the Spilotro character.

Jerry Tarkanian vs. the NCAA — Hired in 1973 as UNLV's head basketball coach, Tarkanian spent most of the following 19 years battling the NCAA over rules violations. Throughout the long battle, his UNLV teams made it to the Final Four on four occasions, winning it all in 1990. During his last 10 seasons, the Runnin' Rebels averaged 31 wins per season.

Rapper Tupac Shakur vs. ? — The hip-hop star was fatally shot September 7, 1996, near the intersection of Flamingo Road and Koval Lane while riding in a BMW driven by Death Row Records' chairman, Marion "Suge" Knight. His murder remains unsolved.

Mike Tyson vs. the masses — While being booed during his introduction at the National Hot Rod Association races at the Las Vegas Motor Speedway in April 2000, the heavy-weight responded by flipping off the crowd and grabbing his crotch. Hey, at least he didn't sing and spit.

 ## FACT OR FICTION?

Mythology has been part of the Las Vegas landscape ever since celebrities and organized crime began arriving in the 1940s. The bigger the stars, the better the stories. To sort out some of the facts from fiction, I went to George Knapp, longtime investigative reporter for KLAS-TV, Channel 8.

Fact or Fiction? Roy Horn of Siegfried & Roy died in the 1980s and was magically replaced by a double.

> ***Knapp:*** "I've had a lot of people call with different scenarios of how Roy died. One included AIDs. Another — and cast members

supposedly were sworn to secrecy on this — involved Roy being crushed by his elephant Gildah and dying in a LaJolla hospital under a different name. I did try to check it out after hearing it so many times over the years, but found absolutely nothing to support it."

Fact or Fiction? The slot machines at McCarran International Airport are looser than most so that visitors are given a positive sendoff.

Knapp: "Fiction. Michael Gaughan has owned the airport franchise and gaming figures show those are very lucrative."

Fact or Fiction? Wayne Newton, who has been around long enough to see every nook and cranny of Las Vegas, told me that he once walked from one Strip property to another by way of a secret tunnel under the Strip.

Knapp: "Haven't heard that one, but Bugsy Siegel supposedly had secret tunnels under the Flamingo." The intriguing possibility was given more credence by a 2002 investigation of subterranean drainage canals by the Las Vegas alternative weekly *CityLife*. During one explorative foray into the Las Vegas underworld, a search team from the publication surfaced near the Imperial Palace's driveway.

Fact or Fiction? Casinos still take cheaters to a back room and bust 'em up.

Knapp: "It wasn't that long ago that it was true. There was a case a few years ago involving Ted Binion and the (Binion's) Horseshoe. While casinos do not routinely beat up suspected cheaters, the people known as 'advantage players,' aka card counters, say they are regularly roughed up and treated badly by security in most major casinos. Card counting is not illegal but the players say they are treated like criminals, often detained illegally and handcuffed, threatened, shoved around and kicked off the property whenever security figures out they are counting cards."

Fact or Fiction? Major Strip properties pump oxygen into the casinos so gamblers will stay awake and play longer.

> **Knapp:** "Fiction." Good thing, I guess, watching how many people fire up cigarettes at the tables.

Fact or Fiction? The mob still runs Vegas.

> **Knapp:** "I would leave that as a question mark. The bent-nose guys are gone, but there are people in law enforcement who believe a new generation of mobster — a laundered mobster, if you will — has replaced the guys that speak in 'dees and dose.' "

Fact or Fiction? *Review-Journal* columnist Ned Day, who frequently made the mob his target, was "hit" by the boys when he drowned while swimming in Hawaii on September 3, 1987.

> **Knapp:** "I still have a little question myself. But all the medical information indicated a heart attack and Ned's family had a history of heart attacks. But Ned told me the mob made runs at him before."

Fact or Fiction? Millions in cash was unaccounted for in the aftermath of the MGM Grand fire in 1980. (I asked Knapp about this because a prominent restaurateur told me he was involved in retrieving "barrels of cash" from the MGM Grand the day after the fire.)

Knapp: "Loren Lomprey was one of the principal investigators for the Clark County Fire Department and is perhaps the most authoritative single source of information on the fire anywhere. I asked him whether he had heard stories about millions of dollars in missing cash and he gave me this answer:

'I've never heard that one, but there were plenty of other myths and rumors. There was a story floating around that two security guards were found dead in the casino cage, still holding burned machine guns, and that they had died protecting the money. Absolutely not true. There was another story that someone had taken an entire wheelbarrow of casino chips out the back door into the alley. I can tell you for a fact that it never happened.

'Without question, huge amounts of money were lost in the fire. Hundreds of slot machines were melted, along with all of the coins inside. Cash was burned up inside the slots of the gaming tables. I know that gaming control agents came in the following afternoon, wearing SCUBA equipment, and went through the casino to secure the remaining casino chips.'"

Fact or Fiction? Steve Wynn is going blind from an incurable disease.

Knapp: "Wynn suffers from retinitis pigmentosa, an inherited, incurable disease that gradually destroys a person's retinas and optic nerve, slowly reducing the field of vision until blindness occurs."

Fact or Fiction? It was mobster Bugsy Siegel's vision to build the Strip's first luxury resort, the Flamingo, in hopes of luring Hollywood's rich and famous to Las Vegas.

Knapp: "The story is part fact, part fiction," says Knapp. "It is well documented that L.A. nightclub operator Billy Wilkerson, a founder of the *Hollywood Reporter*, first came up with the idea for the Flamingo. But Wilkerson ran out of money and Siegel stepped in and took over the project.

"Backed by millions in mob money, Siegel finished the Flamingo in 1946. However, his profligate spending and notorious mismanagement led to suspicion among his silent partners in the underworld. They came to believe that Siegel was skimming from them. Bugsy was gunned down in Los Angeles, a mere six months after the Flamingo finally opened. A team of mob associates assumed control of the Flamingo just minutes after Bugsy's untimely demise."

Special Mention: It is fiction that a boozed-up Shecky Greene, after crashing his car into the fountains at newly opened Caesars Palace in 1966, quipped, "No spray wax."

"It was a Buddy Hackett line, which both comedians used in retelling the story," according to *Review-Journal* entertainment writer Mike Weatherford in his book, *Cult Vegas: The Weirdest, the Wildest, the Swingin'est Town on Earth!* According to the book, all Greene remembers saying is, "I guess I'm arrested."

Bally's — This is where the former MGM Grand stood, before it was gutted by fire on November 21, 1980, in perhaps the most devastating event in Las Vegas history. There were 88 casualties in the disaster. Post-fire legislation made Las Vegas hotels among the safest in the world.

Ted Binion's home — His body was found at 2804 Palomino Lane, the apparent victim of a murder plot, on September 17, 1998. After a sensational trial, Sandy Murphy, Binion's girl-friend and a former stripper, and Rick Tabish, an acquaintance of Binion's, were sentenced to life in prison during national coverage on *Court TV*. She was freed in December 2003, out on $250,000 bail while awaiting an October retrial.

Econo Lodge — Mohammed al-Amir al-Sayed Atta, one of 19 terrorists responsible for hijacking the commercial airliners that flew into the World Trade Center and Pentagon, stayed at this motel, 1150 Las Vegas Blvd. South, on June 30, July 1 and August 13, 2001, *Review-Journal* columnist John L. Smith exclusively reported one week after 9-11. Authorities believe Atta was at the controls of American Airlines Flight 11, a Boeing 767 en route from Boston to Los Angeles that slammed into the World Trade Center's north tower.

Hard Rock Hotel, Suite 658 — John Entwistle, bassist for the legendary rock group The Who, was found dead June 27, 2002, after partying with a stripper on the eve of the band's tour stop at the Hard Rock. His death cancelled the show, an $800,000 deal for the group.

Lake Video store — Dana Plato, the troubled former child star of the sitcom *Diff'rent Strokes*, was arrested after robbing the store on Lake East Drive for $164 in February 1991. She was disguised in a hat, coat and sunglasses, brandishing a pellet gun. Las Vegas singer Wayne Newton posted the $13,000 bail. Plato's troubles eventually got the better of her and she died in 1999. Had she lived, she might have appreciated the fact that the video store is now the Nevada Theatre Company, a home to local actors.

Flamingo Las Vegas — Mobster Bugsy Siegel raised $6 million in mob money in 1945 to fund his diamond-in-the-rough, the Flamingo Hotel and Casino. After a shaky start, the Flamingo played a crucial role in turning Las Vegas into an international destination for gambling and entertainment. Bugsy wasn't around to see it. He had rubbed the Big Boys the wrong way and was killed in Los Angeles in June 1947.

East Sahara Avenue restaurant parking lot — Mob front-man Frank "Lefty" Rosenthal survived a 1982 car bombing in the 600 block of East Sahara Avenue, a parking lot between Marie Callender's and Tony Roma's restaurants.

Oasis Motel — David Strickland, a cast member of Brooke Shields' NBC sitcom *Suddenly Susan*, was found dead, hanging from a bed sheet, in Room 20 of this motel, 1731 Las Vegas Blvd. South, on March 22, 1999. Before taking his life, Strickland had been seen partying with comedian Andy Dick at Glitter Gulch, a seedy downtown topless bar.

Flamingo Road and Koval Lane — Rapper Tupac Shakur was fatally shot September 7, 1996, near this intersection while riding in a BMW driven by Death Row Records Chairman Marion "Suge" Knight. The murder remains unsolved.

Wynn Las Vegas — The site of Steve Wynn's new mega-resort, formerly the Desert Inn, is where Howard Hughes stayed in seclusion and self-imposed squalor from Thanksgiving 1966 to November 5, 1970.

 WHAT HAPPENED TO.... ?

The Dunes? Home of the first bare bosom stage in Sin City, the Dunes was imploded on October 27, 1993, to make room for the Bellagio, Steve Wynn's $1.6 billion mega-resort.

The Elvis suite at the Hilton Hotel? Elvis stayed in the 30th-floor suite between 1969 and 1976. After his death in 1977, the Hilton would, on occasion, charge $5 to those who wanted a tour of the suite. It was torn down to make way for the three high-roller penthouse suites. The new suites were built for $45 million in 1995.

Howard Hughes' Landmark tower? The casino opened July 4, 1969, as the tallest building in Las Vegas (297 feet, six inches) — Hughes made sure of that. He wanted to tweak Kirk Kerkorian, who had just built The International (now the Hilton Las Vegas), by not only having a taller structure but opening the casino before his rival had a chance to pop the champagne. Hughes succeeded. The International made its debut July 30, 1969.

Paul Anka's Jubilation nightclub? One of the bouncers was a big guy by the name of Steve Schirripa, who became the Riviera's comedy club host and, eventually, its manager. From there, he joined HBO's *The Sopranos* as Bobby Baccala. Jubilation later became a long-running nightspot called The Shark Club and is currently a four-acre parking lot adjacent to the Polo Towers, which sits just off the Strip. The Marriott corporation has announced plans to turn the lot into an 840-suite time-share property called The Chateau.

"The Teenbeat Club?" Many a teenager got their first taste of rock 'n roll in the 1960s at this popular nightspot owned by a young entrepreneur. Steve Miller went on to become a Las Vegas city councilman and his club later became Club Paradise, one of the hottest strip clubs in town due, in part, to its location across the street from the Hard Rock Hotel.

Gennifer Flowers? After an unsuccessful radio talk-show in Denver, Bill Clinton's former squeeze spent much of the 1990s in Las Vegas. An accomplished singer, she would join jazz-piano legend Buddy Greco at the Kitchen Cafe to sing a couple of her favorites, including "The Lady is a Tramp" and "Since I Fell for You." She eventually moved on to New Orleans and in early 2002 opened Gennifer Flowers' Kelsto Club in the French Quarter. She has hinted about bringing a show back to Las Vegas, where she was once disinvited from a charity event.

Tower of Pizza? Many Las Vegans remember it as a Sinatra after-show hangout. The site of the former restaurant lies just south of the nightclub

Seven, formerly the Country Star, at Las Vegas Boulevard and Harmon Avenue.

El Rancho Vegas? It was the first hotel on what was then Highway 91, the road to Los Angeles. Now that stretch of road is known as the world-famous Strip.

When it opened on April 3, 1941, at what is now Sahara Avenue and Las Vegas Boulevard, the El Rancho's rooms were only $4 a night but the hotel was considered a premier showcase. When it burned down on June 17, 1960, it was one of the city's worst disasters to that date. The lot has stood vacant for years and sticks out as the biggest parcel of undeveloped land on the Strip.

Corrine Sidney, then married to Sands' impresario Jack Entratter, remembers the night the El Rancho burned down:

"We were having drinks with Frank Sinatra and he said, 'Let's go see a fire.' We didn't have any idea what he was talking about," she said. Sure enough, when they drove down to the El Rancho it soon went up in flames. Frank had underworld connections?! Who knew?

Jerry Tarkanian? A Las Vegas institution as recognizable as some of the Strip's big-names of yesteryear, the towel-chewing Tarkanian retired March 15, 2002, after 38 seasons as a collegiate basketball head coach. His last seven years were at the helm of Fresno State, his alma mater, after his glory years at UNLV.

In 30 seasons of Division I coaching Tark compiled a career 778-202 record and was only the twelfth coach to reach 700 career wins. During his 19 years as head coach at UNLV, the Rebels reached the NCAA Final Four on four occasions: 1977, 1987, 1990 and 1991. The 1990 Runnin' Rebels won it all.

He's back in Las Vegas— although he never really left — attending UNLV games and living the retirement life.

The Rat Pack? First to go was Peter Lawford. Disowned by Frank Sinatra after the Kennedy administration put distance between JFK and Sinatra's mobbed-up reputation, Lawford took a hard fall. He slid into drug and alcohol dependence, and died December 24, 1984, at age 61 in Los Angeles, reportedly of cirrhosis of the liver. Sammy Davis Jr. struggled with throat cancer and died May 16, 1990, at age 64. Dean Martin never got over the death of his son, Dean Paul, in a 1987 jet crash and died a mentally broken man on Christmas Day, 1995, at age 78. The epitaph on his crypt at Westwood Memorial Park in Los Angeles reads: "Everybody Loves Somebody Sometime," which was, of course, his No. 1 hit in 1964 and the theme song of his long-running TV show. Sinatra performed until 1995. He died of a heart attack at age 82 on May 14, 1998. Properties along the Strip dimmed their lights in memory of Davis, Martin and Sinatra after each died. The only other times that happened was for JFK and Ronald Reagan. Joey Bishop, the Rat Pack's chief joke writer and only teetotaler, outlasted them all. He celebrated his 86th birthday on February 3, 2004, at his home in Newport Beach, California.

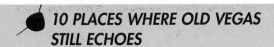

10 PLACES WHERE OLD VEGAS STILL ECHOES

Given the rapid rate of "implosions" and redevelopment in Las Vegas, it's somewhat risky to include this list. Still, a few landmarks have escaped the wrecking ball and showed no signs of being in imminent danger.

Fremont Street — No trip to Las Vegas is complete without visiting the street where it all started in 1905. Nevada's first gaming license was issued to the Northern Club at 15 E. Fremont Street in 1931, the year gaming was legalized. Neon came along in the 1930s, as well, transforming downtown in to "Glitter Gulch." Check out the Golden Gate, famous for its shrimp cocktail, and the Neon Museum (731 South 4th Street), which has been preserving yesteryear neon signs since 1996, offers walking tours. Call **702-229-5366**.

Binion's Horseshoe — Benny Binion and his bigger-than-Texas personality (and reputation) took over the reins of the Horseshoe in 1951, when Las Vegas had less than 20,000 dusty souls. He made the casino a destination spot, first with his display of $1 million and later with his World Series of Poker. But these are lean years for the Horseshoe, which was temporarily forced to close its doors in 2004 before being purchased by Harrah's. Binion's beloved World Series of Poker appears to be headed for Harrah's on the Strip.

El Portal Theater — Fremont Street's El Portal movie theater was a downtown hotspot in its day, when Hollywood-style premieres were staged there. Among them: the 1956 MGM musical

Meet Me in Las Vegas, starring Dan Dailey and Cyd Charisse, with a slew of cameos by Las Vegas stars-in-the-making, including Frank and Sammy. Sinatra was front and center a year later at the El Portal for the opening of *The Joker is Wild*, a movies in which he sang his Oscar-winning "All the Way" while starring as the legendary comedian Joe E. Lewis. The theater itself is a gift shop now but the distinctive outdoor neon sign has survived.

The Golden Steer — "Name anybody and they've been here," says Joe Kludjian, longtime owner of the city's oldest steakhouse, established in 1958. He can back up the bragging. Dean Martin always got Booth No. 6, and band leader Harry James and his actress wife Betty Grable would come in, "but never talked to each other." Joe DiMaggio wanted a seat facing the door so he could see who was coming in. And any time mobster Anthony "The Ant" Spilotro and his FBI tormenter Joseph Yablonsky stopped in, they "would sit and glare across the room at each other." 308 W. Sahara Ave.

Hilton Las Vegas (Formerly The International) — Anyone who knows anything about Elvis realizes that the rebirth of his career occurred on July 31, 1969. It was the date he opened at The International's 2,000-seat showroom, the largest room in town. As I write this, Elvis impersonator Trent Carlini has reclaimed the room for much of 2004 with his tribute "The Dream King." 3000 Paradise Road South.

Wayne Newton at the Stardust Hotel — The Wayner is as Old Vegas as it gets and still one of the top showmen in town. His voice isn't what it used to be, but it matters not to a crowd that comes to see a local legend.

Huntridge Theater — It was opened on October 10, 1944, by film star Irene Dunne and, for a brief time, Loretta Young was a partner. Headliners included Marlene Dietrich, Vincent Price and Abbott & Costello. It was the scene of many a first date and family fun for generations.1208 E. Charleston Blvd.

Piero's Italian Ristorante — Mobster Anthony "Tony the Ant" Spilotro often huddled upstairs in the 1970s and 1980s when it was the Villa D'Este Supper Club.

Chef David Alenik of Pasta Shop Ristorante recalls that his first job in Las Vegas was at Villa d'Este which was owned and operated by Joe Pignatella (a.k.a. Joe the Pig), the former driver and personal chef to Sam Giancana of Chicago mob fame, and also personal chef of Frank Sinatra.

"I will never forget when I first saw Tony Spilotro. He came in the back door flanked by Herbie "Fat Herbie" Blitzstein, his right-hand man. My co-workers mentioned to me that he was the notorious head of the Las Vegas mob, which I laughed off in disbelief. He was 5-feet-5 in shoes, kind of chubby. I soon came to believe. He came in often through the back door just for takeout, always being followed by the FBI in their cars, and he would always drop me a $50 toke.

"They would often have their 'meetings' at lunch time when we were closed. I was trusted to be the only non-member to be allowed in the dining room as I was helping to serve lunch, and they were in full conversation yet I could hardly hear a word they were saying.

"He enjoyed the classic Chicken Vesuvio and drank mostly bottled water. One time I was in the walk-in cooler to get a case of Romaine lettuce, and Joe and Tony came storming in and grabbed the case of Romaine, reached inside, and pulled out $25,000 wadded up in Saran wrap, and told me, 'Kid, that's the most expensive case of Romaine you will ever see.'" 355 Convention Center Drive.

Vegas Vic — The 40-foot-high neon cowboy has held sway over Glitter Gulch since he was erected atop the Pioneer Club in 1951. Mike Zapler of the *Review-Journal* wrote: "San Francisco columnist Herb Caen, now deceased, once joked that while Vic's voice bellowed 'Howdy, Partner,' his wink said, 'Howdy, Sucker.'" Vic was silenced in 1966 when actors Lee Marvin and Woody Strode complained about him during a stay at the Mint hotel. They were filming *The Professionals* at nearby Valley of Fire State Park. Fremont Street Pedestrian Mall

The Moulin Rouge — Listen closely and you can hear the faint murmurs of Sinatra, Sammy, Pearl and Louie. Owner-host Joe Louis is in the house, too. The Moulin Rouge, the first integrated hotel-casino in Las Vegas, opened on May 24,1955, and was closed by November. Black entertainers who could play on the Strip but couldn't sleep or eat there, stayed at the Moulin Rouge. An after-hours magnet, the shows were the stuff of Las Vegas legend. A suspicious fire ravaged the national historic site on May 29, 2003. In 1979 or early 1980, while looking for lodging down the street from the *Review-Journal* (while on AP assignment,) I spent a mostly sleepless night at the Moulin Rouge when it was a rowdy motel. 900 W. Bonanza Road.

"Let me tell you something about Amarillo Slim. There are two things in Texas, steers and queers, and I have yet to see any horns on that country cowboy." — Bob Stupak, after losing in poker to Amarillo Slim.

"See you at Piero's tonight, John." — Sandy Murphy. So certain she was going to be acquitted of murdering Horseshoe casino heir Ted Binion, Murphy set up dinner plans with her defense attorney John Momot on May 8, 2000, the day the jury went out. Eleven days later she was convicted and sentenced to 22 years in prison. She was freed in December 2003, out on $250,000 bail while awaiting an October retrial.

"Texas Dolly is hotter than a widow-woman's love." — Amarillo Slim, on fellow poker icon Doyle (Texas Dolly) Brunson.

"Conceit is God's gift to the sports book." — "Sonny" Reizner, bookmaker.

"You'll never get ahead trying to get even." — "Sonny" Reizner, bookmaker.

"You want to take the guy to the cleaners one shirt at a time." — Bob Martin, bookmaker.

"Pork chops will grow on the palm trees of Tel Aviv before we let Mike Tyson fight Lennox Lewis on HBO." — Showtime executive Jay Larkin. The networks worked out a groundbreaking joint agreement for the June 8, 2002 fight in Memphis.

"I've had an erection for seven months. I've been using it as a hat rack but that's all I've used it for." — Jerry Lewis, during a morning show interview with Las Vegas' KLAS-TV, Channel 8 co-anchors Casey Smith and Alison McCarthy. Lewis, 77, was promoting a pain relief device that made him feel tingly all over.

"Frank who?" — Carl Cohen, Desert Inn casino manager, after knocking crowns off Frank Sinatra's two front teeth. The enraged singer was denied credit (at Howard Hughes instruction) and went on a rampage that ended in a confrontation with the 250-pound Cohen. (From Richard Hack's book *Hughes: The Private Diaries, Memos and Letters.*)

"When you bet on a mortal lock cinch, always save a little cab fare." — Union Plaza owner Jackie Gaughan. A former Omaha bookie, Gaughan once put everything he had on the outcome of the 1948 presidential race. Gaughan's advice may date back to that election. "He bet it all on Thomas Dewey," says son, Michael Gaughan, chairman of Coast Casinos.

Chapter 8

The Sporting Life

Beyond the neon, there's more to Sin City than gambling, entertainment and fancy food. Some of the most spectacular golf courses in the country are in the Las Vegas area, and not all of them require a small house payment to play. And, boxing expert Al Bernstein weighs in on his Top 10 fights.

Contributed by Kevin Iole, *Review-Journal* golf writer.

Bali Hai Golf Club — Billy Walters' course on the Strip is a diamond in the desert. This is truly one of the state's most scenic tracks with its 4,000 palm trees, more than 100,000 tropical plants and flowers, and white crushed granite that makes the sand traps pop out like snowbanks amid the emerald fairways. **702-450-8000**

Cascata — Park Place Entertainment's high-roller course for preferred casino players and guests sits near Boulder City, among red rock canyons and desert vistas. The $52-million course was baptized by Rene Angelil, husband and manager of Celine Dion, who was given the honor of being its inaugural player. A $100,000 credit line reportedly guarantees a starting time. It's so exclusive, the telephone number is unlisted. **www.parkplace.com.**

Primm Valley — This gem was built in 1998 on the Nevada-California border, about 45 minutes south of Las Vegas. It has two Tom Fazio-designed layouts among desert landscaping and lakes. Both have been named to *Golf* magazine's "Top 100 Courses You Can Play." **800-386-7867**

Reflection Bay at Hyatt Regency Lake Las Vegas Resort — This is the first signature resort course in Nevada designed by golf icon Jack Nicklaus. Not long after Reflection Bay opened, *Golf* magazine ranked it among its 1999 "*Top 10 You Can Play*." **702-567-1234**

Rio Secco — This is the Rio's private slice of heaven for its high rollers. No. 9 is already the stuff of legends: Tiger Woods has already reached the green on the 634-yard, par five in two, using an iron. **702-889-2400**

Royal Links — Billy Walters spent millions constructing Royal Links, an homage to some of the great golf holes in the British Open rotation. Voted among *Golf* magazine's *"Top 10 New Courses to Play."* **702-450-8000**

Shadow Creek — What do you get for your $500 greens fee? The ultimate golf experience, some say. *Golf* rated Shadow Creek the 10th-best public course in the country. The *Robb Report*, in its *"Best of the Best"* issue, named it best in the world. Some 20,000 mature trees block out the view of any desert except the surrounding mountains. When casino developer Steve Wynn built it, you needed his personal invitation to play. Now it's available to all guests of MGM-Mirage hotels willing to pay the price. **702-791-7161** or **888-778-3387**

Southern Highlands — Southern Highlands immediately joined the country's elite private clubs when it opened in early 2000. It was co-designed by the father-son team of Robert Trent Jones Sr. and Jr. President and owner Gary Goett wanted his own old-fashioned stamp on the layout, and delivered it with special touches such as pine trees rather than palms. **702-263-1000**

South Shore at Lake Las Vegas — Lake Las Vegas' first course, the private South Shore Golf Club, was named one of the 10 best new private courses in the country by *Golf Digest* magazine. **702-558-0020**

TPC Summerlin — This is where Tiger Woods clinched his first PGA win in 1996. It continues to be part of the annual PGA Tour. **702-256-0222**

One to watch for: The beloved **Desert Inn** course is undergoing a dramatic transformation as part of Steve Wynn's grand plan for his new Wynn Las Vegas. It is due to open in 2005. **702-733-7431**

 ## POPULAR PUBLIC COURSES

Contributed by Tim Dahlberg, Las Vegas-based golf and boxing writer for Associated Press.

Angel Park — Two 18-hole courses plus a lighted par-3 "Cloud Nine" and an 18-hole putting course make this a favorite of locals and tourists alike. **702-254-4653**

Badlands — Like desert golf? This course has holes that skirt canyons and force players to carry shots. A Johnny Miller design, it has some intriguing holes. Translation: Bring extra balls. **702-363-0754**

Bali Hai — The most convenient course for visitors on the Strip, it lies just south of Mandalay Bay. It's pricey and under the path of airplanes from McCarran International Airport, but it's also a forgiving and fun layout. **702-450-8000**

Bear's Best — This new course west of the Strip features the best holes of Jack Nicklaus. Good and tough, and you have to hire a caddie. **702-804-8500**

Boulder Creek Country Club — This Boulder City course opened in 2003 to rave reviews. The semi-private course offers 27 holes of great golf, well worth the short drive. **702-293-9236**

Desert Pines Golf Club — This course just east of downtown has a North Carolina feel, with holes winding between groves of pine trees. It's a little tight, but you use every club here. **702-888-397-2499**

Las Vegas National — Built in the early '60s, it was once the host of the Sahara Invitational PGA tournament. A nice design and convenient location near the Strip add to the appeal. **702-382-4653**

Paiute — It's a hike to get to the location 20 miles north of downtown, but well worth it for three Pete Dye designs in a spectacular desert setting. Try the "Wolf," the latest and best of the three. **702-658-1400**

Reflection Bay — A Nicklaus design at Lake Las Vegas offers spectacular views and even better golf. **702-740-4653**

Royal Links — It's been voted one of *Golf* magazine's "*Top 10 New Courses.*" Think of Scotland in the desert. This course replicates some of the great holes of British Open courses, the "Postage Stamp" and "Road Hole" among them. **702-450-8000**

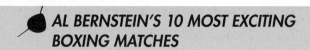
Boxing expert Al Bernstein was hired in 1981 as an ESPN fight analyst for the cable network's weekly boxing series. The Chicago native left ESPN in 2003 to become an analyst for *Showtime Championship Boxing*. He is now a Las Vegan and host of the *Al Bernstein Sports Party* on KBAD-AM 920.

Marvin Hagler defeats Tommy Hearns, KO 3, April 15, 1985, Las Vegas — I called this pay-per-view fight, and it turned out to be three of the greatest rounds in middleweight history. Suffering from bad cuts that threatened to end his run as champion, Hagler took matters into his own hands and knocked Hearns out.

Riddick Bowe defeats Evander Holyfield, W 12, November 13, 1992, Las Vegas — One of the best heavyweight fights ever. Holyfield gave away lots of weight and height, but battled fiercely. The 11th round was magnificent. In the end, Bowe simply wore Evander down.

Muhammad Ali defeats Joe Frazier, KO 14, October 1, 1975, Manilla — A play in three parts. The first five rounds belonged to Ali, and Frazier looked like a shopworn fighter. Then Frazier showed his true grit and came on to batter Ali for the next six rounds. After that, Ali surged again until Eddie Futch, Frazier's trainer, stopped the fight.

Aaron Pryor defeats Alexis Arguello, TKO 14, November 22, 1982, Miami — A battle of yin and yang — the tall, slender, serene Arguello against the shorter perpetual-motion machine that was Pryor. They battled intensely and Pryor took right hands that should have knocked a building down. Eventually he got to Arguello in the 14th.

Larry Holmes defeats Ken Norton, June 9, 1978, Las Vegas — In his first title defense, Norton faced the best contender in Larry Holmes. They produced a classic match. It was almost dead even going into the 15th. That round is considered one of the five best in heavyweight history. Holmes won a razor thin split decision.

Archie Moore defeats Yvon Durelle, KO 11, December 10, 1958, Montreal — This was a knock-down, drag-out fight in which both men tasted the canvas. Ultimately, the Old Mongoose came out the victor.

Michael Carbajal defeats Humberto (Chiquita) Gonzalez, KO 7, March 13, 1993, Las Vegas — In this long-awaited match of two bantamweight champs, Carbajal came off the canvas to knock out Gonzales in a wild slugfest. Gonzales would later change his tactics and box against Carbajal to win two more matches against him.

George Foreman defeats Ron Lyle, KO 5, January 24, 1976, Las Vegas — Both men went down so much they looked punch-drunk until, finally, it was Lyle who stayed down. A brutal display of power from both men.

Frazier defeats Ali, W 15, March 8, 1971, New York — The first meeting of these two icons was as much a historical event as a boxing match. But make no mistake, it was a great boxing match. Frazier's 14th- round knockdown of Ali cemented the decision and the heavyweight title.

Carmen Basilio defeats "Sugar" Ray Robinson, W 15, September 23, 1957, New York

— In an era of great middleweight matches this one was the best. Ironically, the best fighter of all time actually lost. Robinson did eventually come back to beat Basilio to regain his title.

 "LET'S GET READY TO RUMBLE"

Boxing announcer Michael Buffer, a Las Vegas fight fixture, has taken his signature call to venues across the world. Here are 10 events where you might have heard him.

— A special AMWAY gala in front of 15,000 distributors in Atlanta.

— A bar mitzvah in Philadelphia.

— Bass-fishing tournaments. Bull-riding championship events.

— The 1999 Indianapolis 500, where 400,000 heard him substitute, "Ladies and gentlemen, start your engines."

— NBA playoff games.

— A major religious convention, with a minister on one side next to a costumed devil. Some 5,000 conventioneers went bonkers as Buffer delivered the unorthodox invocation, intimidating the beezelbub out of the devil.

— Professional wrestling matches.

— On West German radio stations, where his disco version of "Let's Get Ready to Rumble" was on the Top 20 hit parade for 19 weeks.

— On the Ready 2 Rumble Electronic Boxing Ring toy by Manley Toy Quest. Buffer's "rumble" phrase can be heard before the eight-inch-high action figures duke it out. Buffer charges $15,000 per event. Buffer Enterprises is based in Marina del Rey, California; **bruce@letsrumble.com**.

PRO ATHLETES WHO CALL VEGAS HOME

Thanks to the *Review-Journal* sports staff for helping out with this one. Those listed had to live here long enough for Las Vegas to be considered their primary residence.

Greg Maddux — Maddux, Major League Baseball's first four-time Cy Young award winner, grew up in Las Vegas. He is a Valley High School graduate.

Andre Agassi — The Las Vegas native became only the fifth player in history to win all four of tennis' Grand Slams. His Iranian-born father Mike Agassi was an Olympic boxer in 1948 and 1952. Agassi lives with his wife, tennis icon Steffi Graf, their son Jaden Gil, and their daughter Jaz Elle.

Randall Cunningham — One of UNLV's greatest athletes, Cunningham led the Philadelphia Eagles to the NFC East title in 1988 and to playoff appearances in 1989, 1990 and 1992. He sat out 1996, but came back in 1997 to join Minnesota as a backup. He had his best season in 1998, leading the Vikings to the NFC championship game. He officially retired in 2002 with the NFL's all-time rushing record for a quarterback.

Larry Johnson — Johnson was dominating the middle when UNLV went 69-6 in his two seasons, won the 1990 NCAA basketball championship, and reached the Final Four semifinals in 1991. He was the first player taken. (by Charlotte) in the 1991 NBA draft, and played 10 seasons, averaging 16.2 points per game.

Matt Williams — He was UNLV's all-time homerun leader, with 58 over three seasons. (1984-86) Williams continued with a solid major league career with the San Francisco Giants, Cleveland Indians and Arizona Diamondbacks. A five-time All-Star, he retired in 2003 with 378 homers.

Reggie Theus — Before Larry Johnson there was Reggie Theus. He led UNLV to its first NCAA Final Four in 1977, then went on to play with six NBA teams.

Gerald Riggs — This three-time Pro Bowl running back started his career at Las Vegas' Bonanza High School before attending Arizona State. The Atlanta Falcons made him the ninth over-all pick in 1982 and he rewarded them by becoming their all-time leading rusher with 6,631 yards.

Jim Colbert — Colbert won six events on the men's golf tour before becoming a force on the Senior PGA Tour, twice finishing as the leading money winner (in 1995 and 1996).

David Humm — This standout at Las Vegas' Bishop Gorman High School was the most recruited athlete in Nevada history. Humm was personally courted by the likes of Alabama coach Bear Bryant and Notre Dame's Ara Parseghian. Joe

Namath and Bryant came to Las Vegas, and took Humm to see Paul Anka. Humm was a star quarterback at Nebraska and spent 10 years in the NFL.

Stacey Augmon — This defensive giant from UNLV's national championship basketball team holds records for most games played and most games started. He also tied Greg Anthony for steals. He was the ninth overall selection in the 1991 NBA draft, taken by the Atlanta Hawks.

 ## BEST RACE AND SPORTS BOOKS

Contributed by Jeff Simpson, former *Review-Journal* gaming writer.

Bellagio — The soft, brown leather recliners are the best sports book chairs on the Strip, bar none. The sports book and the adjacent Starting Gate bar are great spots to take a few friends to watch a game. The Snacks fast-food outlet, around the corner from the book, has some of the tastiest quick bites in the city.

Las Vegas Hilton — Discounted football bets on Thursday evenings allow savvy bettors to cut the house edge in half. Convenient parking means quick access, and the Vegas Subs outlet sells fantastic Atlantic City-style sandwiches.

Stardust — Many of the Strip's old-time bettors still make this classic Vegas book their gambling home. For years this was the place that originated the lines other books followed. It still has a research library on site, and a star-studded, weekly expert football-handicapping contest.

The Mirage — It was the Strip's first ultra-luxury book, but the race side is a bit nicer than the sports side, which falls short on supplying big television screens. Race fans, however, have it made. The nearby California Pizza Kitchen provides quick food.

Mandalay Bay — A good snack bar and a broadcast studio for nationally-syndicated sports radio shows are among the highlights of one of the Strip's biggest and nicest books.

Caesars Palace — It's a bit small compared to newer books but maintains a high energy level, particularly during the NCAA basketball tournament or Las Vegas fight nights. It has a good snack bar, too.

Imperial Palace — The hotel is low budget, but the sports book stands apart with the best variety of bets on most major sporting events. The IP famously posts hundreds of unusual proposition bets during each Super Bowl, and takes advance college football wagers every summer.

Bally's — Once a movie theater and then a comedy club, this amphitheater-shaped book is one of the best places on the Strip to watch horse races. Bally's hosts big events each year for the Kentucky Derby and Breeders Cup. Other pluses: a neighboring food court, nearby sports book parking, and proximity to the hotel's monorail station.

Sunset Station — This large and popular off-Strip location in Henderson features a number of giant video screens and several good fast food outlets.

New York-New York — The book is small and seemingly tucked into a hallway. But it's next to the ESPN Zone restaurant and bar, a great place to watch a game after getting your bets down.

 VEGAS FACTOID (Swarming Defense)

One of the most bizarre scenes in the history of the National Hockey League played out in Las Vegas in 1991. Playing in 100-degree temperatures on an outdoor rink behind Caesars Palace, Wayne Gretzky, captain of the Los Angeles Kings, scored the winning goal. But not before the rink's moisture attracted an unnatural assembly of thirsty grasshoppers.

"That was weird," recalled Gretzky, shuddering at the memory of skating over the crunchy critters.

Chapter 9

Because I Get Asked

This chapter covers questions I frequently field — along with some opinions I volunteer unsolicited — about nearly every topic under the desert sun. Questions like where to pop the question? Or equally important, where to find the ultimate strawberry milkshake? Or, where do you get cool stuff like the Elvis glasses with sideburns?

... (or) In My Humble Opinion

Dale Chihuly's glass chandelier — The indoor showpiece of the Bellagio; this amazing multi-colored glasswork hanging over the lobby cost hotel developer Steve Wynn $10 million back in 1998.

Dancing fountains of the Bellagio — While you're at the hotel, don't miss the most magical attraction on the Strip. The fountains start dancing at 3 p.m. weekdays and noon on weekends, but save them for an evening viewing. Remember, they do not operate when it's windy.

Wynn Las Vegas — This might be our safest Top 10 pick in the book. Steve Wynn has been promising his $2.6 billion transformation of the former Desert inn will be "the Bellagio times 10" when it opens in April 2005. Wynn loves water attractions. His showcase feature will be a 150-foot mountain with a five story waterfall cascading into a lake.

View from the ghostbar — The best panoramic view of the Strip is from the "55th floor" (thanks to some creative numbering) observatory deck atop the Palms.

Grand Canyon flyover — You can drive there, but it's four times closer by air. Several tour companies offer a spectacular and reasonably priced birds-eye view of Mother Nature's best production.

View from the House of Blues Foundation Room — You haven't seen Las Vegas until you've seen it from this indoor/outdoor perch on top of Mandalay Bay. Alas, it's a private club on any day but Monday.

Mamma Mia! — Mandalay Bay's ABBA musical is the best feel-good show on the Strip. The last 15 minutes might be the most uplifting in show business.

Mystere — Treasure Island's older sister show of *O*, without the water.

O — They dance, they dive, they swim. And you'll swoon over this artistic aquatic extravaganza.

Stratosphere Tower — A view of Vegas from the clouds, more than 1,000 feet up, plus thrill rides galore.

 TOP 10 PLACES TO PROPOSE (non-restaurant)

Every night in Las Vegas is Valentine's Day for lovers, so here are some special places for that special occasion.

Any patio fronting the Bellagio's dancing fountains at night — For this, they should charge admission.

Bellagio lobby — Under Dale Chihuly's $10 million floral glasswork, of course.

Bellagio Conservatory — If you're into hearts and flowers, and a grand setting for a photo of the big moment, this is paradise.

Eiffel Tower — A 360-degree observation deck on Paris Las Vegas' scale-model tribute to the famous monument offers a breathtaking view of the Strip from 50 stories up.

Venetian Grand Canal gondola ride — Get into the flow with a romantic, operatic tune from a gondolier.

ghostbar's outdoor observatory deck at the Palms — It's probably not for you if you're afraid of heights, or ghosts. But, hey, proposing is way scarier.

Secret Garden of Siegfried & Roy — Home of the German illusionists' big cat family in a jungle setting.

The Rio's Voodoo Lounge patio — With the Palms' ghostbar sometimes selling "passes" to cut the line and Mandalay Bay's House of Blues Foundation Room requiring a membership, the comparable views at this older club might be more accessible for lovers with no time to waste.

Stratosphere Tower — The view looking down the Las Vegas Strip's river of neon is a sight to (have and) behold.

Pontevecchio Bridge at Ritz-Carlton — It's off the Strip by 17 miles, but worth the drive, especially on a full-moon night.

 BEST FREEBIES

Admittedly, Las Vegas isn't in a "bargain" phase when it comes to room rates or restaurants. It's nonetheless aware of the need to keep its edge over the gaming competition in nearly every state now, and so it still offers some spectacular "comps" you won't find on the riverboat.

Bellagio dancing fountains — The most photographed site in Las Vegas is truly the Land of "Ah-h-h's."

Bellagio Conservatory — You can go back at least four times because the floral theme changes with the seasons.

Casino Legends Hall of Fame — The Tropicana's museum offers videos of Old Vegas, costumes of Liberace and Elvis, celebrity contracts and paychecks from the 1950s. All you need for entry are coupons that can be found throughout the hotel and in the giveaway magazines.

Circus Circus big top shows — Aerial acts and jugglers amid the slot machines is a tradition dating back to 1968 in the first fully-themed casino. The free shows are on the second-floor concourse every 45 minutes.

Fremont Street Experience — Watch spectacular light-and-sound shows under a 90-foot steel canopy that spans three blocks. The computer-generated underwent a major upgrade in 2004.

Cook E. Jarr — We're not woofin' on this pick. Late-night crowds have been been diggin' Jarr's throwback act for 20 years. When he's not barking up business for Harrah's Carnival Court on Tuesdays and Wednesdays, 11 p.m. - 1 a.m., he's running with his pals Tom Jones and Bill Medley. See you there, dawg. Harrah's. **702-369-5000**

Masquerade in the Sky — The Rio offers a Mardi Gras parade several times each day, complete with live performers and parade floats suspended from an overhead track.

The Mirage Volcano — Wasn't it just yesterday when this was the hottest tourist attraction on the Strip?

"The Sirens of TI" — Check out the sexy female stars and new, racier approach to the pirate battle, formerly the Battle of Buccaneer Bay, that debuted to mark the hotel's 10th anniversary in October 2003.

Bobby Barrett — The Frank Sinatra sound-alike was uprooted from his longtime home when the MGM's Brown Derby folded, but he's worth perusing the lounge listings to find.

 PLAYING THE TOURIST

No matter how long one lives here, we're all tourists in a city that re-invents itself every few years. These sights are worth a first or fifth visit.

Downtown — It all started here in Glitter Gulch, and the canopied Fremont Street Experience has been a major boost in bringing tourists back downtown. Call **702-678-5600** to get the schedule for the canopy's animated light show.

Ethel M's Chocolate Factory — Ethel Mars was the mother of Forrest Mars, creator of the chocolate dynasty that included Mars Bar, Milky Way, 3 Musketeers, Snickers and M&Ms. There's a cactus garden next door

to this candy factory named in her honor.
2 Cactus Garden drive at Sunset Way and
& Mountain Vista Street, Henderson/Green
Valley. **702-433-2500 www.ethelm.com**

Grand Canyon — Las Vegas offers the closest major airport to this marvel of nature. You can see it from the ground or remember the faster option of small planes and helicopters, the latter making scheduled landings in prime scenic areas.

Helicopter tours by night — Anyone can feel like a high roller by taking a nightly flight down the neon valley known as the Strip.

Hoover Dam and Lake Mead — Construction of Hoover Dam in the 1930s spurred growth in Las Vegas and led to legalized gambling. Lake Mead is the area's top outdoor recreational playground.

Liberace Museum — It's as campy as Vegas gets, but this treasure trove of rhinestones, sequins, furs and rare pianos captures the verve of the world's greatest showman. 1775 E. Tropicana Ave.. **702-798-5595**

Red Rock Canyon Conservation Area — Travel 20 miles from the Strip to another world, one of world-class rock climbing and hiking.

Stratosphere Tower — The city's tallest tower at 1,149 feet, offers a grand view of the Strip and city sprawl.

Wedding Chapel tour — With almost 50 chapels now operating in the marriage capital of the world, there are tours that take you past the good, bad and the cheesey.

Valley of Fire State Park — A moonscape of eroded sandstone and sand dunes more than 150 million years old can be found about 50 miles northeast of Las Vegas off Interstate 15. The valley is so named because the brilliant rock formations appear to be on fire under the scorching sun.

 NORM'S DECADENT DOZEN

Las Vegas is all about guilty pleasures and most of these flashed through my mind during a 10-hour stay in the Clark County Detention Center in September 2003 (all charges were dropped after my blood alcohol level came back as 0.00). There I experienced what I thought was surely the worst lunch in this hemisphere: two individually wrapped slices of processed cheese, two slices of white bread and two scoops of suspect chicken salad. Then I remembered the Tijuana Jail (assignment) and its gagging gruel.

Strawberry milkshakes at The Mad Greek — O.K., Baker, California, isn't exactly in Las Vegas. But millions pass through on the Las Vegas-Los Angeles I-15 corridor. Fresh sliced strawberries make this sinfully rich treat the ultimate milkshake.

Coconut crème brulee at Pink Ginger — This twist on the popular baked custard was the dessert find of 2003. Chef Ryan Fahey of the Flamingo's restaurant served it in split coconuts and topped it with fresh berries and toasted coconut.

Dover sole at Michael's — The Barbary Coast's gourmet room serves what just might be the world's most exquisite piece of fish.

Pineapple mojitos at Fix — Nitro on the rocks.

Pig sandwich at NASCAR Café — Perfect sauce, tasty lean pork. I'm betting you will agree this specialty from the Sahara's themed restaurant takes home the bacon. A true pigout.

Fire-roasted jerk shrimp at Bahama Breeze — A sizzling skillet of shrimp flavored with Caribbean spices makes for one of the best bar-food discoveries in years at this fun eatery, part of the Flamingo Road "restaurant row" in the Hughes Center office park.

Pastilla at Marrakech — A heavenly puff pastry consisting of peaches, apples and nuts and covered with powdered sugar is served at this Middle Eastern restaurant, where you can sit on floor pillows or belly dance the calories away.

Prime strip steak at Del Frisco's Double Eagle Steak House — I was a ribeye kind of guy until Montana beefeater Kent Rockwell put me on to Del Frisco's 16-ounce strip.

Chilled strawberry soup at Picasso — The secret ingredient to this intense and glorious fruit dessert? All you need is Mother Nature. Chef Julian Serrano tells me he takes 10 pounds of strawberries, leaves them out at room temperature and forgets about them for 4-to-5 hours. "When they get warm, they drip," he said. The result is strawberry juice in its purest form.

Margaritas (no salt) at the Pink Taco — Consumer warning: After two of these specialties inside the Hard Rock Hotel's Mexican cantina, I was half-blind. Of course, for me, it's a shorter trip .

Sterling Brunch at Bally's — The ultimate foodie experience. Yes, it's pushing 60 bucks, but where in the world can you have a spread for that price that includes, for starters, lobster tail, sturgeon caviar, beef tenderloin, fresh sushi and Cordon Rouge champagne? A mind-boggling feast.

Wolfgang Puck's Oscar Night Smoked Salmon Pizza — The gold standard by which all pizza must be measured. Puck has turned this into a beloved fixture at Hollywood's top Oscar parties. Ingredients: lox-style salmon, diced red onion, diced cucumber, capers and sour cream, all crowned with caviar. It's served at all Puck eateries.

 TOP 10 EVENTS

Andre Agassi's "Grand Slam for Children" — Vegas' own tennis icon raises millions every fall (usually the last Saturday in September) with an assist from celebrity entertainer friends such as Elton John, Billy Joel, Stevie Wonder and Robin Williams.

Billboard Music Awards — The music industry gathers in February at the MGM Grand to honors its top sellers. The result: one of the biggest celeb-fests of the year.

CineVegas Film Festival — Launched in 1998, this week-long movie marathon has bounced around town, but lately seems to have found a permanent home at Palms resort and its Brendan Theatres.

Elvis Extravaganza Impersonator Contest — This three-day event in early January is prime people-watching territory at the Westward Ho.

Invensys Classic at Las Vegas — Formerly the Las Vegas Open, this is the PGA tour's highest-paying event, with $4.5 million paid out in prize money and $765,000 of that going to the first-place winner.

Las Vegas International Marathon — About 8,000 runners arrive in early February to compete in this half-marathon and 5K run on the old Los Angeles Highway.

Las Vegas 400 NASCAR Winston Cup Race — More than 115,00 people pack into the Las Vegas Motor Speedway for the championship race on the first weekend of March, creating a small city of their own and making this the biggest annual sporting event on the West Coast.

National Finals Rodeo — Cowboys conquer the Strip every December, converging upon the Thomas & Mack Center for the Super Bowl of rodeo. Tickets are coveted for the 10-day event, which draws about 170,000 people to watch the best rodeo performers compete for a $4.5 million purse.

New Year's Eve — One of the world's largest outdoor parties, the Strip has attracted up to

250,000 revelers. And it wasn't until 2000 that they even had fireworks to watch. A disappointing "millennium" celebration in 1999 led the major Strip properties to co-ordinate a synchronized rocket-launch from their rooftops.

Professional Bull Riders Tour — The top 45 bull riders compete during four days in October for a purse of $1 million at the Thomas & Mack Center. In 2004, the event was to become even larger and expand into a second venue, the Mandalay Bay Events Center.

 TOP 10 COOLEST SOUVENIRS

Baseball caps with lighted antlers — The perfect gift for a Las Vegas Christmas can be found amid the many distractions of the Bonanza World's Largest Gift Shop, 2400 Las Vegas Blvd. South.

"Blue Viagra" fudge — You don't need a prescription for this chocolate concoction made with Amaretto, vanilla and blue food coloring. It's a rare day when a shopper won't approach the display case and ask, in a low voice, "Does this really work?" Management at Bonanza General Store has copyrighted the concoction. A card inside reads: "We make no nutritional or medical claims." So hold the jokes. The staff has heard them all.

Camoulfludge — The Bonanza General Store's mix of peanut butter and chocolate uses food coloring as a secret weapon for that brown-and-tan warfare color. In 1991, during Operation Desert Storm, an order for 15 pounds of the stuff was received from the Pentagon.

Dice clock — The grand champion of Vegas kitsch is one of the most popular items at the Bonanza World's Largest Gift Shop and similar knick-knack stores.

Eiffel Tower-shaped glass — Bon vivants can drink up from a replica of the replica for $12.50 at Paris Las Vegas's Le Petit Bar.

Elvis glasses with sideburns — Anyone can be a Vegas Elvis with these accessories from the Bonanza World's Largest Gift Shop.

Elvis clocks with swinging legs — Because sometimes the glasses and sideburns just aren't enough. It's also at Bonanza World's Largest Gift Shop.

Elvis driver's license — No self-respecting Elvis fan would leave Las Vegas without one. Bonanza World's Largest Gift Shop.

Elvis bumper sticker that reads: "Thank you, thank you very much" — That's what you'll be hearing when you take all these goodies home. Bonanza World's Largest Gift Shop.

The Stratoblaster glass — Your Eiffel tower glass might look lonely on the shelf without this plastic replica of the Stratosphere, topped with a straw that looks like the roller coaster at the top of the tower.

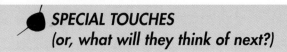

SPECIAL TOUCHES
(or, what will they think of next?)

The elevator to the Eiffel Tower restaurant opens to a view of the kitchen, allowing arriving diners to see soufflés popping out of the oven, strawberries being dipped in a sugar glaze and dessert plates being prepared with chocolate replicas of the Eiffel Tower.

Hugo's Cellar, the gourmet restaurant at the Four Queens, provides a red rose to all female dinner guests. They order 150 a night on weekends.

The complimentary whipped potatos at Nobhill in the MGM Grand come in six flavors: roasted garlic, lobster, French Raclette cheese, black truffles, corn and fennel. They're served in a six-section copper serving pan.

The Palms bachelor suites include a stripper pole, along with a small dance floor and synchronized strobe lights.

Picasso's prodigious floral buffet on the centerpiece credenza. The Bellagio reportedly budgets $12,000 to $15,000 a month for fresh flowers at its crown-jewel restaurant.

Trumpeters hail the presence of the bride, who stands on a balcony above the **Ritz-Carlton's Florentine Gardens**. The bride lowers a love letter to her intended, then descends a grand staircase as the trumpets announce her arrival at the wedding site in the garden. Doves or butterflies are optional in the $6,000 package.

The Ritz-Carlton's stargazing program covers all the bases. There's "Stars & Cigars" night for the older crowd and "Stars and S'Mores" night for the kids.

The Scintas' meet-and-greet autograph session after each show. The Rio's family band is one of the few headlining acts on the Strip to be so accessible.

Hair stylists and make-up artists are provided to the model-servers at Tabu, the MGM Grand nightclub, an hour prior to their shifts.

Viva Las Elvis! The Delmonico Steakhouse at The Venetian offers tiny finger sandwiches made with peanut butter and bananas.

 ## THE BEST VIEWS IN TOWN

Keep these vantage points in mind for either the mayhem of New Year's Eve or a calm summer night in the city of lights.

The **Bellagio's Fontana Room** patio looks out over the dancing fountains, with the Eiffel Tower in the background. Just as spectacular is the **Eiffel Tower**, where patrons get a reverse perspective of the Bellagio's lake.

If it's people-watching you prefer, the patio of **Mon Ami Gabi** restaurant at Paris Las Vegas offers sidewalk tables on one of the most-traveled sidewalks in the country.

If vertigo is not an issue, the **Stratosphere Tower** is the ultimate spot to watch a sunset, while **ghostbar** at the **Palms** offers the best panoramic view of the Strip, complete with a clear acrylic panel to stand on and look straight down. A less trendy option is the top-floor lounge of the **Polo Towers** time-shares, smack in the middle of the action on the Southern Strip.

Most breathtaking? The **House of Blues' Foundation Room** at Mandalay Bay, but it requires special privilages to get in most nights.

If you prefer to view the lights of the Strip from a suburban distance, go with **Whiskey Beach** at **Green Valley Ranch** in southern Henderson, the balcony at the **J.W. Marriott/Rampart Casino** or the **Summit restaurant** in Sun City, both in the western suburbs of Las Vegas.

Chapter 10

Just for Fun

Tourists have the darndest questions. Just ask the showgirls from Jubilee or the gondoliers at The Venetian. This final chapter will, hopefully, steer you away from getting the locals' knickers in a knot. Plus, we'll take the easy bet and predict you haven't heard these high-roller stories.

MOST ANNOYING QUESTIONS SHOWGIRLS (and one male dancer) GET ASKED

"Do you live in the hotel? — Diane Palm, Jubilee.

"What's your stage name?" — Norma Wood.

"Are your eyelashes real?" — Palm, a reference to the inch-long faux lashes.

"How much do you make in tips?" — Dana Rogers Martin, former lead singer, *Jubilee*.

"Do you get to keep the costumes?"— Shannon Marie Sherman, *Jubilee*.

"What else do you do for a living?" — Holly Moss, *Jubilee*.

"You say you're a dancer and they ask, 'Are you a stripper?'" — Rachel Zinn, *Jubilee*.

"What time do you get off?" — Paula Moore, *Jubilee*.

"Where's the seafood buffet?" — Kimberly Denmark, *Showgirls*.

"What's it like being around topless showgirls all the time?" — Anthony Brown, dancer, *Jubilee*. Answer: "After a while, it's like being around your sister," said Brown, a 13-year Metro patrolman.

GOOFIEST QUESTIONS HEARD BY THE VENETIAN'S GONDOLIERS

"Is that a recording or are you really singing?" — Robert Peterson.

"Is the gondola on a track?" — Dick Martinson.

"Does the gondola go outside?" — Kimberly Brent (The Grand Canal is on the hotel's second floor, and we think it's safe to say there are no current plans to add a flume ride).

"Did you just start singing?" — Craig Thomas, whose singing background includes 11 years of opera training.

"Is that a real accent?" — Tom Cassell, a New York City native who was raised Italian (He also plays the thug Dominic Fabrizi in *Tony & Tina's Wedding* at the Rio).

"Did The Venetian send you to Venice to learn how to be a gondolier?" — Martinson.

"Do you own the gondola?" — Brent.

"How do I get back to The Venetian from here?" — Brent.

"Which boats take me back to my room?" — Brent.

The Frogmen of Lake Bellagio — Like comman-dos on a night mission, three-man teams slip into motorized rubber rafts and prowl Lake Bellagio to keep the dancing fountains in perfect rhythm. When they're not busy troubleshooting the 1,198 water-emitting devices, the certified divers are busy with housekeeping chores. "We've found hats, glasses, cell phones and cameras," said Curtis Hunton, the Bellagio's manager of front features. "We even retrieved a $20,000 Rolex and diamond rings." Oh, if only those waters could talk.

Keeper of the Luxor Sky Beam — John Lichtsteiner oversees the operation of the world's most powerful light, a 42.3 billion-candlepower shaft of light that resembles a stairway to heaven.

Ride operator of the Stratosphere's Big Shot — Ruby Malalay has ridden the top-of-the-world thrill machine more than 1,000 times. "That's my wakeup call. It gets me going," said Malalay, who is still an adrenalin junkie as she approaches 70. She makes the trip as often as 10 times a day.

Sky painters — As long as the Strip's building-boom continues, the sky's the limit for the artists who paint puffy clouds on the ceilings of themed casinos and retail malls.

The Venetian's Grand Canal gondoliers — Yes, some are shipped in from Venice, where they plied the real Grand Canal.

Light-bulb changers — Don't laugh until you've been on patrol with a crew for Young Electric

Sign Co., searching the Strip for outages. They return the next day and ascend the signs, or take hotel elevators to a certain floor and rappel down to the problem area. On a busy day, they change 300 to 400 bulbs. One particularly challenging assignment was installing lights on the Stratosphere's Big Shot thrill ride. The Fremont Street Experience is another major undertaking. "We'd take a 110-foot lift down there," said Steve Weeks, assistant division manager. "Every night after the shows were complete we had four guys who fixed all the outages. There are just short of two million light bulbs in there. . . . Our motto is to get it fixed before our client knows it's out."

Mandalay Bay wave-pool operator — During the pre-opening testing in 1999, Moses Mokuahi didn't part the sea like his namesake, but he did crank up a tsunami of biblical proportions: a 13-foot wall of water that washed away beach furniture and soaked the wedding chapel. "I got everybody's attention," said Makuahi, an ex-surfer from Hawaii. Good thing the executive offices are on high ground or Moses would give "office pool" new meaning.

The dozen scuba divers who spend all of Cirque du Soleil's "O" show underwater — The audience only sees them once, but they're down there to ensure the safety of the performers. They handle rigging and deliver oxygen lines to those who "disappear" underwater.

Aureole's wine angel — Brook Bradbury, dressed in an all-black body suit equipped with bottle holsters, steps into the gourmet restaurant's trademark 42-foot-high glass-enclosed wine tower 40 to 50 times each day. She climbs into a harness, then "floats" up to the bottle of choice. Most asked question: "Is the wine at the top the most expensive?" (Answer: "No.") Another angel, local model Kara Moncrief, is the daughter of city councilwoman Janet Moncrief.

Shills — Some are paid plants in the audience who are called on stage to play along with magic tricks or banter with headliners. Others are given house money to make big bets and encourage more action at a slow craps table. The grand prize has to go to the stripper shill, whose job it is to sit near a large party of men, call over his stripper of choice and, after getting a lap dance deluxe, lavish the dancer with a c-note (using the money she gave him) to encourage bigger tips.

MOST-REQUESTED SINATRA SONGS

Contributed by Sinatra sound-a-like Bobby Barrett.

"The Way You Look Tonight"

"New York, New York"

"My Way"

"Summer Wind"

"Fly Me to the Moon"

"That's Life"

"It Was a Very Good Year"

"Luck Be a Lady"

"The Lady is a Tramp"

"One For my Baby (And One More For The Road)"

 10 SONGS THAT STILL LIGHT UP LAS VEGAS

"Con Te Partiro" — Andrea Bocelli. If you've spent any time in the vicinity of the dancing fountains, you will recognize this as the Bellagio's theme song.

"Everybody Loves Somebody" — Dean Martin. Dino was nicknamed the "Beatle Buster" because he knocked them out of the No. 1 spot with "Everybody" on August 15, 1964.

"The Gambler" — Kenny Rogers. A flop for singer/songwriter Don Schlitz in early 1978, Rogers took it to No.1 after Larry Butler brought it to him. Next to "Viva Las Vegas," it must be the most quoted "Vegas" theme song out there.

"I'll Be Seeing You" — Liberace. And you can still see almost everything Liberace at his Las Vegas museum.

"Luck Be a Lady" — Frank Sinatra. And to think he didn't sing it in the movie of *Guys and Dolls*; Marlon Brando did.

"Mr. Bojangles" — Sammy Davis Jr. He didn't just sing it; he lived it.

Theme from the TV series Vega$ — Here's to you Dan Tanna, the coolest Vegas cat to come along since the Rat Pack.

"That Old Black Magic" — Louie Prima and Keely Smith. Listen closely and you can still hear the echoes from the Sahara's Casbar Lounge.

"This Could be the Start of Something Big" — Steve Lawrence and Eydie Gorme. They still endure as Las Vegas' No. 1 fun couple.

"Viva Las Vagas" — Elvis Presley. Hard to believe the name was an afterthought of the film's director, George Sidney.

10 QUICK WAYS TO PISS OFF THE LOCALS

— Ask if that's "the real Eiffel Tower."

— Ask the cocktail server to smile.

— Blame the dealer's "bad karma."

— Burst into "Viva Las Vegas" for no apparent reason.

— Expect comps because you're an athlete.

— Cross the Strip when the pedestrian light is red.

— Cross the Strip where there is no pedestrian crossing.

— Keep saying, "Prices were never this high when the mob ran Vegas."

— Request to spin the roulette wheel.

— Tell everyone who serves you, "I can't imagine how people actually live in this town."

10 THINGS TO LEAVE AT HOME

— Your spouse. (Just kid-d-d-ing).

— Your Midwestern values.

— Your diet.

— Your sleeping pills.

— Your Speedo.

— Your temper.

— Your attitude.

— Your fear of crowds.

— Your new shoes.

— Your Bible.

 ## SIN CITY RUMORS THAT WON'T GO AWAY

Rumor analysis courtesy of Don Usherson, longtime entertainment writer and publicity man for the old MGM Grand (now Bally's) back in "the day."

Danny Gans is going to quit headlining to do a TV sitcom. Some of us media types think this rumor about the popular impressionist's future once his Mirage gig runs out in 2006 comes directly from his then-personal manager, Chip Lightman. Saying it makes it so? **Usherson:** "It was supposed to be an impersonation of Seinfeld."

Wayne Newton is having vocal cord surgery to restore his voice. Anyone who has heard Mr. Las Vegas lately could see how this one could get started. **Usherson:** "Why? Whose grandmother complained?"

"Colonel" Tom Parker owed the Hilton millions in gambling debts amassed during Elvis' seven-year run there. I asked Wayne Newton about it: "I am told from very reliable sources they (Parker and Elvis) had markers at the Hilton for $35 million. They never expected to collect it." **Usherson:** "Most of the reliable sources that were there when Elvis was alive are dead! That includes Elvis, the Colonel, Dr. Elias Ghanem — Elvis' personal physician here — and Bruce Banke, the Hilton public relations maven for 20 years, who was a confidante of Elvis and the Colonel. Hmmm, perhaps the bathroom custodian is shooting his mouth off again."

Sammy Davis, Jr., considered Linda Lovelace, the infamous porn star, as an opening act for his Las Vegas show. Several biographies have alleged sexual trysts between the overnight porn phenomenon and the showman during his hedonistic days of the early '70s; the most recent is Will Haygood's exhaustive *In Black and White: The Life of Sammy Davis Jr.* The late porn star had her own autobiography, *Ordeal*, in which she claims the singer "did suggest I put together a big Las Vegas act." **Usherson:** "True, it was proposed to him. Whether he was actually considering it, only Sammy knows for sure."

Some of the most beautiful production show dancers are men. Sorry guys, this one is true. **Usherson:** "There have been several. The most well known, I believe, was the singer in *Crazy Girls*, Jahna Steele, whose real name was John Reis. She was voted 'Las Vegas' Sexiest Showgirl' in the mid-1980s before it became widely known she was a transsexual."

The remains of aliens are stored at Area 51. Credit movies such as *Independence Day* for fueling the legend of the top-secret base near Groom Lake. **Usherson:** "Only the *Men in Black* know for sure — and George Knapp (the KLAS-TV, Channel 8 reporter whose investigations have helped popularize the legend)."

Elvis and Ann-Margret had a torrid affair while shooting *Viva Las Vegas* here in 1963. The late director George Sidney, still sharp as a tack before his death in 2002, suggested there was plenty to that rumor. **Usherson:** "I don't think that one rates as a rumor anymore."

Pete Rose came close to being hired by The Palms as a casino host in 2002. **Usherson:** "But I think Palms owner George Maloof was thinking more along the lines of, 'Right after Pete gets into the Baseball Hall of Fame AND the Sacramento Kings win the NBA championship.' "

The annual buzz that the Tropicana and the prime piece of land it sits on is going to be sold, and turned into another mega-resort. **Usherson:** "There's more chance that the Mandalay Bay and MGM Mirage groups will get together to buy the property, implode the building and erect one huge parking facility. Don't laugh. In the late 1970s, MGM (now Bally's), the Dunes (now the Bellagio), Hilton (Flamingo) and Caesars didn't buy the corner lot when they had the chance to buy out the Gaughans and stop the building of another successful competitor, the Barbary Coast. All eventually had to spend a fortune on expansion of their parking facilities and lost a lot of gaming revenue to the Coast Resort people."

 ## TOP 10 SLOGANS FOR LAS VEGAS

Contributed by Rob Johnson, Denver-based actor, writer and comedian.

— "Gateway to bankruptcy court."

— "Food, folks and failed marriages."

— "But it's a dry heat."

— "Mom and dad went to Las Vegas and all I got were these lousy pasties."

— "If you lived here, you'd be broke by now."

— "Come for the gambling, stay for the loan sharks."

— "Mafia-free for 23 days"

— "Over 10 billion dreams shattered."

— "It's Breast Augmentastic."

— "Buffets, buffets, buffets."

You can find white tigers and dolphins in Las Vegas, but nothing causes more excitement here than the "whales," or the Goliaths among high rollers. Only about 200 high rollers qualify as whales, making them a rare species indeed. Here are 10 whale tales:

— A handful of the richest whales routinely play for $200,000 a hand. Australian media mogul Kerry Packer not only regularly bets that much, but has plunked down $200,000 bets for the dealers as a form of a tip.

— Packer is no longer allowed to play at the MGM Grand after taking the house for more than $20 million one night in the late 1990s. He switched to the Bellagio and reportedly lost more than $25 million after September 11, 2001, when the government's no-fly edict forced him to stay too long in Sin City.

— One Asian high roller was so superstitious that he would call his astrologer back in Japan to get a reading on the luckiest hours to gamble.

— Golfer John Daly racked up $2.5 million in slot jackpots in August 2001 before walking with $750,000. Daly usually plays the $100 and $500 slot machines.

— NBA legend Michael Jordan lost $1 million during a weekend and rebounded with a $1 million turnaround on his next trip to town.

— A veteran casino host had a whale who would regularly win or lose $10 million on a trip to Las Vegas. "When I asked him if it bothered him to lose $10 million he said, 'No problem, I only play with the interest.'"

— *Hustler* publisher Larry Flynt reportedly lost $1 million playing blackjack one night, and won it back the next night at the Las Vegas Hilton. When the CBS news magazine *48 Hours* aired the segment, hotel executives didn't like the piece and fired hotel spokesman Tim Chanaud.

— Keeping whales happy is the bottom line. Many a whale who has lost a bundle has been handed the keys to a new Rolls Royce or Ferrari as a token of appreciation.

— A gambler described as a "semi high roller" dropped from sight for several years. One day he called a Las Vegas casino host to say he was coming to town. When he arrived, he was poorly dressed and clearly down and out. "He told me he was working as a fry cook." He came in with a modest bankroll, hoping to recoup, but lost it all. Word later came that he committed suicide.

— One Asian high roller well known in Las Vegas and Atlantic City for his high-limit play gambled with his life — and lost. He was murdered in Japan with a samurai sword after suffering heavy losses with misappropriated organized crime money.

— There was a woman who used to come over from Los Angeles every weekend and lose $5,000 to $10,000. "We'd give her $200 to 300 in airfare, but she'd lose that too," a casino executive recalls. "So we started giving her a plane ticket instead."